AA004131

# CYBER 2025

The Tenth International Conference on Cyber-Technologies and Cyber-Systems

September 28th - October 2nd, 2025

Lisbon, Portugal

**CYBER 2025 Editors**

Steve Chan, Decision Engineering Analysis Laboratory, USA

Hirokazu Hasegawa, National Institute of Informatics, Japan

**Printed from e-media with permission by:**

Curran Associates, Inc.
57 Morehouse Lane
Red Hook, NY 12571

**Some format issues inherent in the e-media version may also appear in this print version.**

Copyright© (2025) by International Academy, Research, and Industry Association (IARIA)
Please refer to the Copyright Information page.

Printed with permission by Curran Associates, Inc. (2025)

International Academy, Research, and Industry Association (IARIA)
412 Derby Way
Wilmington, DE 19810

Phone: (408) 893-6407
Fax: (408) 527-6351

petre@iaria.org

**Additional copies of this publication are available from:**

Curran Associates, Inc.
57 Morehouse Lane
Red Hook, NY 12571 USA
Phone: 845-758-0400
Fax: 845-758-2633
Email: curran@proceedings.com
Web: www.proceedings.com

## Table of Contents

# CYBER 2025

# Forward

The Tenth International Conference on Cyber-Technologies and Cyber-Systems (CYBER 2025), held between September 28$^{th}$, 2025, and October 2$^{nd}$, 2025, in Lisbon, Portugal, continued a series of international events covering many aspects related to cyber-systems and cyber-technologies; it was also intended to illustrate appropriate current academic and industry cyber-system projects, prototypes, and deployed products and services.

The increasing size and complexity of the communications and the networking infrastructures are making difficult the investigation of resiliency, security assessment, safety and crimes. Mobility, anonymity, counterfeiting, are characteristics that add more complexity in Internet of Things and Cloud-based solutions. Cyber-physical systems exhibit a strong link between the computational and physical elements. Techniques for cyber resilience, cyber security, protecting the cyber infrastructure, cyber forensic, and cyber-crimes have been developed and deployed. Some new solutions are nature-inspired and social-inspired, leading to self-secure and self-defending systems. Despite the achievements, security and privacy, disaster management, social forensics, and anomalies/crimes detection are challenges within cyber-systems.

We take here the opportunity to warmly thank all the members of the CYBER 2025 technical program committee, as well as all the reviewers. The creation of such a high-quality conference program would not have been possible without their involvement. We also kindly thank all the authors who dedicated much of their time and effort to contribute to CYBER 2025. We truly believe that, thanks to all these efforts, the final conference program consisted of top-quality contributions. We also thank the members of the CYBER 2025 organizing committee for their help in handling the logistics of this event.

We hope that CYBER 2025 was a successful international forum for the exchange of ideas and results between academia and industry for the promotion of progress in the field of cyber-technologies and cyber-systems.

**CYBER 2025 Chairs**

**CYBER 2025 General Chair**
Steve Chan, Decision Engineering Analysis Laboratory, USA

**CYBER 2025 Steering Committee**
Carla Merkle Westphall, UFSC, Brazil
Barbara Re, University of Camerino, Italy
Rainer Falk, Siemens AG, Corporate Technology, Germany
Daniel Kästner, AbsInt GmbH, Germany
Anne Coull, Flinders University, Adelaide, Australia
Steffen Fries, Siemens, Germany
Sibylle Fröschle, TU Hamburg, Germany
Andreas Aßmuth, Fachhochschule Kiel, Germany
Hirokazu Hasegawa, National Institute of Informatics, Japan

**CYBER 2025 Publicity Chairs**

Laura Garcia, Universidad Politécnica de Cartagena, Spain
Lorena Parra Boronat, Universidad Politécnica de Madrid, Spain
Guman Singh Chauhan, John Tesla Inc, California, USA

# CYBER 2025
# Committee

## CYBER 2025 General Chair

Steve Chan, Decision Engineering Analysis Laboratory, USA

## CYBER 2025 Steering Committee

Carla Merkle Westphall, UFSC, Brazil
Barbara Re, University of Camerino, Italy
Rainer Falk, Siemens AG, Corporate Technology, Germany
Daniel Kästner, AbsInt GmbH, Germany
Anne Coull, Flinders University, Adelaide, Australia
Steffen Fries, Siemens, Germany
Sibylle Fröschle, TU Hamburg, Germany
Andreas Aßmuth, Fachhochschule Kiel, Germany
Hirokazu Hasegawa, National Institute of Informatics, Japan

## CYBER 2025 Publicity Chairs

Laura Garcia, Universidad Politécnica de Cartagena, Spain
Lorena Parra Boronat, Universidad Politécnica de Madrid, Spain
Guman Singh Chauhan, John Tesla Inc, California, USA

## CYBER 2025 Technical Program Committee

Aysajan Abidin, imec-COSIC KU Leuven, Belgium
Shakil Ahmed, Iowa State University, USA
Cuneyt Gurcan Akcora, University of Manitoba, Canada
Oum-El-Kheir Aktouf, Grenoble Institute of Technology, France
Abdullah Al-Alaj, Virginia Wesleyan University, USA
Khalid Alemerien, Tafila Technical University, Jordan
Usman Ali, University of Connecticut, USA
Izzat Alsmadi, Texas A&M, San Antonio, USA
Anas AlSobeh, Southern Illinois University, USA
Alina Andronache, University of West of Scotland, UK
Abdullahi Arabo, University of the West of England, UK
Andreas Aßmuth, Fachhochschule Kiel, Germany
A. Taufiq Asyhari, Coventry University, UK
Syed Badruddoja, University of North Texas, USA
Morgan Barbier, ENSICAEN, France
Samuel Bate, EY, UK
Vincent Beroulle, Univ. Grenoble Alpes, France
Clara Bertolissi, Aix-Marseille University | LIS | CNRS, France
Khurram Bhatti, Information Technology University (ITU), Lahore, Pakistan

Michael Black, University of South Alabama, USA
Davidson R. Boccardo, Clavis Information Security, Brazil
Felix Boes, University of Bonn, Germany
Ravi Borgaonkar, SINTEF Digital / University of Stavanger, Norway
Florent Bruguier, LIRMM | CNRS | University of Montpellier, France
Enrico Cambiaso, Consiglio Nazionale delle Ricerche (CNR), Italy
Nicola Capodieci, University of Modena and Reggio Emilia (UNIMORE), Italy
Pedro Castillejo Parrilla, Technical University of Madrid (UPM), Spain
Steve Chan, Decision Engineering Analysis Laboratory, USA
Christophe Charrier, Normandie Universite, France
Guman Singh Chauhan, John Tesla Inc, California, USA
Bo Chen, Michigan Technological University, USA
Mingwu Chen, Langara College, Canada
Lu Cheng, ArizonaState University, USA
Ioannis Chrysakis, FORTH-ICS, Greece / Ghent University, Belgium
Anastasija Collen, University of Geneva, Switzerland
Giovanni Costa, ICAR-CNR, Italy
Domenico Cotroneo, University of Naples, Italy
Anne Coull, Flinders University, Adelaide, Australia
Monireh Dabaghchian, Morgan State University, USA
Dipanjan Das, University of California, Santa Barbara, USA
João Paulo de Brito Gonçalves, Instituto Federal do Espírito Santo, Brazil
Vincenzo De Angelis, University of Reggio Calabria, Italy
Noel De Palma, University Grenoble Alpes, France
Luigi De Simone, Università degli Studi di Napoli Federico II, Italy
Jerker Delsing, Lulea University of Technology, Sweden
Patrício Domingues, Polytechnic Institute of Leiria, Portugal
Paul Duplys, Robert Bosch GmbH, Germany
Soultana Ellinidou, Cybersecurity Research Center | University Libre de Bruxelles (ULB), Belgium
Rainer Falk, Siemens AG, Corporate Technology, Germany
Omair Faraj, Internet Interdisciplinary Institute (IN3) | UOC, Barcelona, Spain
Eduardo B. Fernandez, Florida Atlantic University, USA
Steffen Fries, Siemens Corporate Technologies, Germany
Somchart Fugkeaw, Thammasat University, Thailand
Damjan Fujs, University of Ljubljana, Slovenia
Steven Furnell, University of Nottingham, UK
Gina Gallegos Garcia, Instituto Politécnico Nacional, Mexico
Tiago Gasiba, Siemens AG, Germany
Huangyi Ge, Purdue University, USA
Hamza Gharsellaoui, National School for Computer Science (ENSI) | University of Manouba, Tunisia
Kambiz Ghazinour, SUNY Canton, USA
Konstantinos Giannoutakis, University of Macedonia, Greece
Uwe Glässer, Simon Fraser University - SFU, Canada
Ruy Jose Guerra Barretto de Queiroz, Federal University of Pernambuco, Brazil
Ekta Gujral, Walmart Global Tech, USA
Chunhui Guo, San Diego State University, USA
Amir M. Hajisadeghi, AmirkabirUniversity of Technology, Iran
Arne Hamann, Robert Bosch GmbH, Germany

Hirokazu Hasegawa, National Institute of Informatics. Japan
Ehsan Hesamifard, University of North Texas, USA
Gahangir Hossain, West Texas A&M University, Canyon, USA
Mehdi Hosseinzadeh, Washington University in St. Louis, USA
Zhen Huang, DePaul University, USA
Maria Francesca Idone, University of Reggio Calabria, Italy
Christos Iliou, Information Technologies Institute | CERTH, Greece / Bournemouth University, UK
Shalabh Jain, Research and Technology Center - Robert Bosch LLC, USA
Kevin Jones, University of Plymouth, UK
Georgios Kambourakis, University of the Aegean - Karlovassi, Samos, Greece
Sayar Karmakar, University of Florida, USA
Dimitris Kavallieros, ITI-CERTH, Greece
Saffija Kasem-Madani, University of Bonn, Germany
Daniel Kästner, AbsInt GmbH, Germany
Basel Katt, Norwegian University of Science and Technology (NTNU), Norway
Mazaher Kianpour, Norwegian University of Science and Technology, Norway
Lucianna Kiffer, Northeastern University, USA
Sotitios Kontogiannis, University of Ioannina, Greece
Tanya Koohpayeh Araghi, University Oberta de Catalunya, Spain
Dragana S. Krstic, University of Nis, Serbia
Uma Kulkarni, Institute for Secure Cyber-Physical Systems | Hamburg University of Technology (TUHH), Germany
Fatih Kurugollu, University of Derby, UK
Cecilia Labrini, University of Reggio Calabria, Italy
Ruggero Lanotte, University of Insubria, Italy
Rafał Leszczyna, Gdansk University of Technology, Poland
Weiran Lin, Carnegie Mellon University, USA
Eirini Liotou, National and Kapodistrian University of Athens, Greece
Jing-Chiou Liou, Kean University - School of Computer Science and Technology, USA
Hao Liu, University of Cincinnati, USA
Xing Liu, Kwantlen Polytechnic University, Canada
Qinghua Lu, CSIRO, Australia
Yi Lu, Queensland University of Technology, Australia
Mahesh Nath Maddumala, Mercyhurst University, Erie, USA
Jorge Maestre Vidal, Universidad Complutense de Madrid, Spain
Louai Maghrabi, Dar Al-Hekma University, Jeddah, Saudi Arabia
Yasamin Mahmoodi, Tübingen University | FZI (Forschungszentrum Informatik), Germany
David Maimon, Georgia State University, USA
Ivan Malakhov, Università Ca' Foscari Venezia, Italy
Timo Malderle, University of Bonn, Germany
Mahdi Manavi, Mirdamad Institute of Higher Education, Iran
Sathiamoorthy Manoharan, University of Auckland, New Zealand
Michael Massoth, Hochschule Darmstadt - University of Applied Sciences / CRISP – Center for Research in Security and Privacy, Darmstadt, Germany
Vasileios Mavroeidis, University of Oslo, Norway
Mohammadreza Mehrabian, University of the Pacific, USA
Weizhi Meng, Lancaster University, UK
Jayakrishna Menon, Arizona State University, USA

Carla Merkle Westphall, UFSC, Brazil
Massimo Merro, University of Verona, Italy
Caroline Moeckel, Open University, UK
Srinivas Murri, Meta, USA
Lorenzo Musarella, University Mediterranea of Reggio Calabria, Italy
Vasudevan Nagendra, Stony Brook University, USA
Roberto Nardone, University Mediterranea of Reggio Calabria, Italy
Niels Nijdam, University of Geneva, Switzerland
Klimis Ntalianis, University of West Attica, Greece
Jason Nurse, University of Kent, UK
Riccardo Ortale, Institute for High Performance Computing and Networking (ICAR) of the National Research Council of Italy (CNR), Italy
Jordi Ortiz, University of Murcia, Spain
Richard E. Overill, King's College London, UK
Mohammad Zavid Parvez, Charles Sturt University, Australia
Antonio Pecchia, University of Sannio, Italy
Eckhard Pfluegel, Kingston University, London, UK
Muhammad Haris Rais, Virginia Commonwealth University, USA
Paweł Rajba, Hitachi Energy / University of Wroclaw, Poland
Massimiliano Rak, Università della Campania, Italy
Alexander Rasin, DePaul University, USA
Danda B. Rawat, Howard University, USA
Barbara Re, University of Camerino, Italy
Leon Reznik, Rochester Institute of Technology, USA
Jan Richling, South Westphalia University of Applied Sciences, Germany
Giulio Rigoni, University of Florence / University of Perugia, Italy
Antonia Russo,University Mediterranea of Reggio Calabria, Italy
Peter Y. A. Ryan, UniversityofLuxembourg, Luxembourg
Florence Sedes, Université Toulouse 3 Paul Sabatier, France
Abhijit Sen, Kwantlen Polytechnic University, Canada
Shirin Haji Amin Shirazi, University of California, Riverside, USA
Srivathsan Srinivasagopalan, AT&T CyberSecurity (Alien Labs), USA
Zhibo Sun, Drexel University, USA
Ciza Thomas, Government of Kerala, India
Zisis Tsiatsikas, Atos Greece / University of the Aegean, Greece
Tobias Urban, Institute for Internet Security - Westphalian University of Applied Sciences, Gelsenkirchen, Germany
Eric MSP Veith, OFFIS e.V. - Institut für Informatik, Germany
Mudit Verma, Arizona State University, Tempe, USA
Simon Vrhovec, University of Maribor, Slovenia
Stefanos Vrochidis, ITI-CERTH, Greece
James Wagner, University of New Orleans, USA
Gang Wang, Emerson Automation Solutions, USA
Qi Wang, Stellar Cyber Inc., USA
Ruoyu "Fish" Wang, Arizona State University, USA
Xianping Wang, Florida Polytechnic University, USA
Zhiyong Wang, Utrecht University, Netherlands
Zhen Xie, JD.com American Technologies Corporation, USA

Cong-Cong Xing, Nicholls State University, USA
Ping Yang, State University of New York at Binghamton, USA
Wuu Yang, National Chiao-Tung University, HsinChu, Taiwan
George O. M. Yee, Aptusinnova Inc. & Carleton University, Ottawa, Canada
Serhii Yevseiev, National Technical University - Kharkiv Polytechnic Institute, Ukraine
Wei You, Renmin University of China, China
Yicheng Zhang, University of California, Irvine, USA
Piotr Zwierzykowski, Poznan University of Technology, Poland

**Copyright Information**

For your reference, this is the text governing the copyright release for material published by IARIA.

The copyright release is a transfer of publication rights, which allows IARIA and its partners to drive the dissemination of the published material. This allows IARIA to give articles increased visibility via distribution, inclusion in libraries, and arrangements for submission to indexes.

I, the undersigned, declare that the article is original, and that I represent the authors of this article in the copyright release matters. If this work has been done as work-for-hire, I have obtained all necessary clearances to execute a copyright release. I hereby irrevocably transfer exclusive copyright for this material to IARIA. I give IARIA permission or reproduce the work in any media format such as, but not limited to, print, digital, or electronic. I give IARIA permission to distribute the materials without restriction to any institutions or individuals. I give IARIA permission to submit the work for inclusion in article repositories as IARIA sees fit.

I, the undersigned, declare that to the best of my knowledge, the article is does not contain libelous or otherwise unlawful contents or invading the right of privacy or infringing on a proprietary right.

Following the copyright release, any circulated version of the article must bear the copyright notice and any header and footer information that IARIA applies to the published article.

IARIA grants royalty-free permission to the authors to disseminate the work, under the above provisions, for any academic, commercial, or industrial use. IARIA grants royalty-free permission to any individuals or institutions to make the article available electronically, online, or in print.

IARIA acknowledges that rights to any algorithm, process, procedure, apparatus, or articles of manufacture remain with the authors and their employers.

I, the undersigned, understand that IARIA will not be liable, in contract, tort (including, without limitation, negligence), pre-contract or other representations (other than fraudulent misrepresentations) or otherwise in connection with the publication of my work.

Exception to the above is made for work-for-hire performed while employed by the government. In that case, copyright to the material remains with the said government. The rightful owners (authors and government entity) grant unlimited and unrestricted permission to IARIA, IARIA's contractors, and IARIA's partners to further distribute the work.

# The Domain Name Life Cycle as an Attack Surface: Systematic Threat Mapping and Defense Recommendations

Thomas Fritzler and Michael Massoth
Hochschule Darmstadt (h_da) - University of Applied Sciences
member of European University of Technology (EUt+)
Department of Computer Science
Darmstadt, Germany
email: thomas@fritzler.me, michael.massoth@h-da.de

*Abstract*—**This paper presents a phase-based security analysis of the domain-name life cycle - pre-registration, active registration, expiry, and malicious re-registration. Synthesizing peer-reviewed studies, documented incidents, and current threat intelligence (2014-2025), we map key attack vectors (for example typosquatting, dangling records, registrar compromise, expired-domain abuse) to concrete mitigations (registrar hardening, zone hygiene, renewal governance). The result is a concise model and a threat-to-control table aimed at practitioners in enterprises and registrars. This is a conceptual, literature-based synthesis; no new measurements are introduced. We argue that domain names are critical security assets that require continuous management across technical and administrative controls.**

***Keywords-Domain Life Cycle; Domain Security; Domain Management; Expired Domains; Cybersecurity Best Practices.***

## I. Introduction

Domain names form the backbone of navigation on the Internet. They function both as a company's **digital identity** and as **trusted anchors** for users accessing web resources [1]. A compromised domain can therefore trigger wide-ranging consequences - from phishing attacks to the complete takeover of online services. Attackers systematically exploit these weaknesses by operating with legitimate domains or deceptively similar names in order to bypass security mechanisms. In doing so, virtually every attack that relies on a seemingly legitimate sender or web address to evade defenses is facilitated [2].

Against this backdrop, the present paper analyzes the **vulnerabilities throughout the entire life cycle of a domain** - from registration, through operation and expiration, to potential takeover by third parties. The objective is to highlight *technical attack vectors* and *documented incidents* for each phase and to demonstrate their relevance for enterprises. To this end, existing scientific studies, security reports, and recorded attacks are comparatively evaluated. In addition, well-established tools are presented that can help to detect and prevent such weaknesses. **This contribution is a conceptual, literature-based synthesis rather than an empirical measurement study.** We address the following research questions (RQs): **RQ1** - What threats emerge at each phase of the domain name life cycle? **RQ2** - Which technical and organizational controls effectively mitigate them? **RQ3** - Which gaps suggest directions for future empirical validation?

The remainder of this paper is structured as follows: **Section II** reviews related work and outlines our methodology; **Section III** presents the phase-oriented model of the domain name life cycle and a consistent, phase-by-phase threat mapping; **Section IV** discusses implications, provides concrete recommendations, states limitations, and outlines future work.

## II. Related Work

Prior studies typically focus on isolated threat surfaces. Typosquatting and other naming-confusion attacks have been analyzed in depth [3][4], while the risks of dangling Domain Name System (DNS) records [5][6] and expired-domain takeovers [7] have been explored separately. Adjibi *et al.* extend this line of research by quantifying how the Fortune 500 pursue *defensive registrations* and showing that roughly three-quarters of look-alike domains remain under third-party control [1]. Their work highlights a critical blind spot - corporate protection tends to begin *after* registration - and therefore does not capture threats that arise *before* or *after* that window (e.g., pre-registration brand monitoring or post-expiration abuse). **In contrast to prior work, this paper systematically maps threats across all four phases and couples them with phase-specific mitigations for practitioners.**

Other surveys take a broader perspective on DNS security. Schmid provides a view on systemic threats in DNS Insecurity [8], while Ramdas *et al.* catalog mitigation techniques against DNS-related attacks [9]. Affinito *et al.* examine domain lifetimes and quantify baseline risks across the ecosystem [10]. However, none of these works integrates security threats across the *entire domain life cycle*.

**Methodology:** We conducted a structured literature scan (2014-2025) across ACM DL, IEEE Xplore, USENIX, NDSS and selected industry reports. Inclusion: peer-reviewed security work on DNS/domain life cycle, empirical incident reports; Exclusion: marketing/duplicate blog posts. Search keys included "domain life cycle security", "dangling DNS", "expired domains", "typosquatting", "registrar hijacking". Two reviewers screened titles/abstracts; we extracted threats, affected life cycle phase, and mitigation classes. This is a conceptual synthesis without new measurements.

Despite these valuable contributions, the literature still lacks an integrated framework that maps vulnerabilities from pre-registration to post-expiration. This paper closes that gap by

TABLE I. COMPARATIVE OVERVIEW OF EXISTING REVIEWS AND HOW THIS WORK DIFFERS

| Work | Focus/Method | Life cycle coverage | Added value of this paper |
|---|---|---|---|
| COMST'21 [8] | Broad DNS threats survey | Cross-cutting; not phase-based | End-to-end, phase-based map (P1-P4) with aligned mitigations |
| ICCS'19 [9] | DNS attack mitigations (short survey) | General DNS; no life cycle lens | Life cycle view + concrete phase-wise controls |
| TMA'22 [10] | Domain lifetimes / expiry risks | Emphasis on lifetime/expiry | Integrates pre-reg, active, expiry, re-reg threats |
| NDSS'25 [1] | Defensive registrations (Fortune 500) | Narrow pre/post around reg. | Complements with ops/expiry abuse beyond registration |

proposing a phase-oriented security model and by deriving unified mitigation guidelines that link technical, administrative, and policy controls.

## III. Domain Life Cycle and Its Vulnerabilities

The life cycle of a domain can be simplified into four phases: **(1) Pre-registration**, **(2) Active Registration**, **(3) Expired Domains**, and **(4) Malicious Re-registration**. While Phase 3 resembles Phase 1 in terms of availability, residual references (e.g., third-party logins, old references to email addresses, or inbound links) may still exist. Each phase poses distinct security threats [10]. *Per phase, we (i) define scope, (ii) enumerate threats, (iii) list recent evidence, and (iv) summarize mitigations.* Table II summarizes the key threats and defenses across the four phases addressed in this work. The following subsections outline these phases and their typical weaknesses.

### A. Phase 1: Pre-registration

In the first phase, a domain is completely **freely available** - either never registered before or released by its previous owner - and can be registered anew. Even though no legitimate content exists under such a name, attackers can still **abuse** it by proactively registering it [11].

**T1. Typosquatting and look-alike domains:** Typosquatting refers to registering domain names that are **confusingly similar** to a well-known brand, usually through typographical errors or minor spelling changes. Users who mistype or fail to notice the difference are silently routed to the wrong site. This technique has deceived users since the early commercial Internet. Typical variants include letter transpositions, character omission or insertion, or using **homographs** - visually similar characters from other scripts. A well-known early case was `goggle.com`, intended to mislead visitors to `google.com`. Modern attackers increasingly rely on Internationalized Domain Names (IDNs) that mix, e.g., Cyrillic and Latin letters - an attack most browsers now detect and block [12].

Despite longstanding defensive efforts, typosquatting remains highly prevalent and continues to evolve. Recent incidents show that this **scheme continues to flourish** and evolve. In 2024, for example, a security vendor reported a surge of Bifrost-Trojan campaigns leveraging VMware typosquats [13]. Fraudulent job sites and even parts of the SolarWinds supply-chain attack also traced back to typosquatting domains [14]. An Akamai analysis found that about 20.1% of all newly observed domains it tracks - roughly 13 million malicious domains every month, i.e., well over three million each week - are flagged as malicious, many of them look-alike registrations [15]. These are not accidental errors but **deliberate registrations by criminals**. The technique now underpins sophisticated fraud schemes, such as combining bogus websites with matching social-media profiles, intercepting emails (e.g., Business-Email-Compromise), or smuggling trojanized code into development environments. One example is the discovery of Python libraries like `"requessts"` or `"reqquests"`, typosquats of popular packages registered on look-alike domains to trick developers [3].

*a) Example: the Mastercard typo:* A real-world incident underscoring the danger of small DNS errors is the *Mastercard typo*. A **faulty** DNS entry went unnoticed for years, meaning attackers could have registered the misspelled domain and weaponized it [16]. The case shows that even an innocuous typo in a DNS zone can open major security gaps, because customers or internal systems may unknowingly resolve the "wrong" domain.

*b) Example: the BYD domain confusion:* A recent real-world incident illustrates how brand visibility can backfire when obvious look-alike domains are left unprotected. During UEFA EURO 2024, Chinese electric-vehicle maker BYD bought prominent pitch-side advertising. Curious spectators naturally tried the German country code Top Level Domain (ccTLD) variant `byd.de` - but that name was already owned by an unrelated adult-toy retailer. The unexpected spotlight drove a massive traffic spike to the site, forcing its owners to publish a disclaimer that they were not affiliated with the car company [17]. The episode shows that even legitimate marketing can funnel large crowds to misleading domains, creating fertile ground for fraud or malware if criminals register similar names first. Careful domain-portfolio management across relevant TLDs is therefore essential throughout the life cycle of a brand.

Scientific studies confirm typosquatting's breadth. A 2014 USENIX study analyzing hundreds of thousands of domains found that typosquatting is **widespread** and growing [4]. Actors invest significant resources to monetize these domains. More recent surveys reveal that **74% of look-alike domains** targeting Fortune 500 companies are held by third parties [1], highlighting aggressive coverage by criminals and domain speculators. Such names are often used for **phishing**, fraud, or brand abuse.

**T2. Orphaned and published domains:** A threat that spans **Phase 1 (Pre-registration)**, also surfaces during **Phase 2 (Active Registration)** through abandoned or misconfigured *subdomains*, and re-appears in **Phase 4 (Malicious Re-registration)**. Attackers actively look for **domain or subdomain names that are still referenced** - in documentation, configuration files, code snippets, or lingering DNS records - yet are either unclaimed or left dangling. Although these names look legitimate from the outside, they are **not actually under the rightful owner's control**. By claiming an orphaned domain or subdomain, adversaries can invisibly insert themselves into traffic intended for the original destination [5][18][19]. Modern scanners such as *BadDNS* now crawl websites to locate externally referenced, takeover-able domains [20].

### B. *Phase 2: Active Registration*

In Phase 2 the domain is under **active ownership** (typically by an organization) and used for services such as websites, email, or Application Programming Interface (APIs). Although the name is legitimately controlled, numerous **attack vectors arise from misconfiguration or insufficient safeguards**. The main concerns are **DNS configuration**, registrar security, and subdomain management [2].

**T1. DNS Misconfigurations and Gaps:** A domain is only as secure as its DNS settings. Faulty or negligent configuration can give adversaries opportunities to abuse or manipulate the name. Key issues include:

**Missing DNSSEC signing:** Domain Name System Security Extensions (DNSSEC) cryptographically signs DNS responses to guarantee their **authenticity and integrity**. Without DNSSEC, domains are vulnerable to cache-poisoning and manipulation - an attacker could inject forged answers and redirect users to malicious IPs. Despite clear benefits, adoption remains low: an APNIC study in 2023 found that **only about 4.3 % of .com domains are DNSSEC-signed** [21]. In other words, more than 95 % lack this protection. Some TLDs fare better - `.nl` reaches roughly 60 % coverage [21] - yet a global gap persists. Technical complexity, operational effort, and limited know-how leave many domains exposed whenever an attacker can influence a resolver or intercept traffic.

**Missing CAA records:** A **CAA (Certification Authority Authorization)** record lets owners specify which CAs may issue TLS certificates for the domain. Without CAA, any CA could issue a certificate (assuming domain-control checks can be bypassed via DNS tampering or error). CAA therefore reduces the risk of *unintended or fraudulent issuance*. Nevertheless, a 2020 survey showed that **only about 3 % of the Alexa Top-1-Million** domains publish a CAA record. Given the ease of deployment, this figure is strikingly low. A CAA record might restrict issuance to `Let's Encrypt` or `DigiCert`; some domains even use `issue ";"` to permit **no** CA - 358 cases in that study. [22]

**Open zone transfers (AXFR):** Zone transfers replicate data between authoritative name servers. If a server is misconfigured to allow AXFR from *unauthorized IPs*, attackers can pull a **complete zone dump**. The dump reveals all records - internal subdomains, IP mappings, etc. - and aids further attacks. Although CVE-1999-0532 highlights the risk, Internet scans as late as 2016 still found "large numbers" of exposed servers. Successful leaks expose hidden services such as `vpn.company.com` or `dev.db.company.com`. Mitigation is trivial: allow transfers **only to authorized secondary servers** [23].

**Stale or incorrect DNS records:** Domains or subdomains often move or services are retired without cleaning all records. Such **stale entries** may point nowhere - or worse, be taken over (see *subdomain takeover*). A special case is **incorrect NS entries**: if registry-level name servers are misspelled or unresponsive, the domain becomes unstable. Attackers have exploited these situations. The 2024 *"Sitting Ducks"* campaign revealed hundreds of thousands of domains with **DNS misconfigurations** (e.g., bad NS pointers) effectively abandoned [24]. Attackers impersonated the intended name servers and seized control [24]. Infoblox found nearly **800,000 vulnerable domains** in three months; about 9 % (>70,000) were **actively hijacked** [24]. These domains - often legitimate but misconfigured - were then abused for phishing, investment fraud, and more [24]. Even a minor lapse (e.g., an outdated NS entry) can turn a domain into *easy prey*.

A common scenario is a DNS record that points to an external domain (e.g., via **CNAME**, **MX**, or **NS**) no longer controlled by the organization. Such a **dangling record** invites abuse: registering the missing domain diverts traffic to the attacker. For instance, `example.com` might include `oldservice.example.com CNAME oldservice-provider.com`, even though `oldservice-provider.com` no longer exists. Whoever registers that domain gains control over every request to `oldservice.example.com`. The same applies to unregistered domains listed as **MX** or **NS**, enabling email interception or name-server takeover [5][19].

In short, during Phase 2 the owner must ensure that all security-relevant DNS settings are correct and current. Misconfiguration directly threatens the **integrity of name resolution**. Additional precautions include avoiding unnecessary internal disclosures (e.g., chatty TXT records or revealing subdomain names) and routinely auditing the zone for **anomalous entries**.

**T2. Threats from subdomain takeover:** Many organizations delegate subdomains to external cloud providers - e.g., `shop.example.com` for SaaS or `cdn.example.com` for a CDN - via **CNAME** records (such as `shop.example.com CNAME shopsaas.com`). While the service is active and configured, no issue arises. **The threat arises when external services are decommissioned but DNS entries remain.** The subdomain then points to a *non-existent* target - a *dangling DNS record*. Attackers can **re-register** or claim that resource (e.g., the freed **cloud host name or account**) to seize control [5][19]. This is known as a **subdomain takeover**. The attacker "captures" a victim's subdomain by obtaining the referenced external domain or resource. Once in control, they can serve content or intercept traffic under the trusted hostname. Cloud platforms are frequent targets: Azure Web Apps, AWS S3 buckets, GitHub Pages, Heroku, and more. If the CNAME is left behind after deletion, an attacker can spin up an identically named service and **take over** the subdomain [5][19].

Empirical work shows subdomain takeover is not rare but a **systemic risk**: in 2016 researchers identified 467 vulnerable subdomains among the Alexa Top-10k plus university sites [6]. Follow-up scans across cloud platforms found over **700 000 vulnerable DNS entries** overall [5][7].

Root causes are usually poor cleanup: projects end, services migrate, yet DNS records linger. Especially in DevOps and cloud cultures where teams create subdomains autonomously, visibility is lost. Companies should schedule **regular audits** of their DNS zones to detect *dangling* entries. Tools such as **Subjack**, **Subzy**, takeover modules in scanners like **Nuclei**, or the comprehensive **BadDNS** can automate detection by checking CNAME/MX/NS targets for registrability [20].

**T3. Weaknesses in Registrar Security:** Domain protection also depends heavily on the **security of the registrar account** - the portal where the name is registered and managed. An attacker who gains access can **seize the entire domain**: redirect name servers, change ownership details, or transfer the domain to another account.

Numerous incidents of **domain hijacking** stem from social engineering or registrar breaches. Attackers exploit weak passwords, absent two-factor authentication, or technical flaws at smaller registrars. A prominent example is the **"Sea Turtle"** campaign (2017-2019), in which a state-sponsored actor compromised registrars and DNS providers to hijack high-profile domains - mainly in the Middle East - by phishing credentials and altering DNS to their own servers, even acquiring valid TLS certificates [25]. This illustrates that even perfectly configured DNS zones fail if **registrar infrastructure is breached**.

Cyber-criminals without state backing also hijack domains. Often they first compromise the owner's email address (e.g., by registering an expired domain from Phase 3), then trigger a **password reset**. Support staff may also be fooled into **unauthorized transfers**. High-value domains - famous brands or premium .com generics - regularly appear in news reports after such thefts [25]. In 2015, for instance, Lenovo's domain was redirected to a defacement server, allegedly via registrar account compromise [26].

Key **weak points** include absent **multi-factor authentication**, lack of **Registry Lock** (a service that blocks critical changes unless manually approved), and poor credential hygiene. Registry Lock is highly effective yet mainly adopted by large firms: **46 % of companies using enterprise registrars** employ it, versus only 7 % using mass-market registrars. Many SMEs may not know or purchase the feature, and some registrars do not actively promote it [27].

Altogether, Phase 2 requires a **holistic defense** of the domain: both technical DNS parameters and administrative access must be secured, or attackers may gain total control - with potentially catastrophic outcomes such as fraud, reputation damage, or data breaches.

### *C. Phase 3: Expired Domains*

Domains are typically registered for periods of 1 to 2 years and must be renewed regularly. If a domain is **not renewed in time**, it enters an expiry workflow. The registrar first places it in a short **grace period** (typically 30-45 days, during which the original holder can recover it for a fee), optionally followed by a **redemption period** (another ~30 days, usually with a higher restoration fee). Finally, the domain is deleted and released for **re-registration** [10]. From a corporate perspective, allowing a domain to lapse is usually unintentional, yet still occurs frequently, whether through organizational errors (missed reminder emails, staff changes) or because the name is deemed no longer important (e.g., after rebranding or project shutdown). Older corporate domains or those of acquired subsidiaries are especially prone to "slipping through" [28]. Once a domain becomes available, attackers have an excellent opportunity to register and exploit it. Phase 3 therefore shows the threats posed by **expired domains**.

**T1. Abuse of expired domains for phishing and fraud:** A **released domain** can be registered by anyone - professional domain traders (*drop-catchers*) often run automated scripts to acquire attractive names the moment they drop. Criminal actors monitor such drop lists for **promising targets**. Domains previously owned by well-known organizations are highly valuable because they **inspire trust**. Attackers re-register them and deploy **convincing replicas** of the original content to deceive users. A typical pattern is launching a **fake webshop** on a formerly legitimate domain [29]. Brian Krebs [30] chronicled how a photographer's lapsed portfolio domain was re-registered by fraudsters and converted into a counterfeit sneaker store. Visitors seeking her work unknowingly entered card details, which criminals harvested and resold. Besides reputational damage, the photographer lost access to linked accounts because attackers also seized her former email address [29]. Automated renewal management and systematic SaaS deprovisioning ensure that critical domains never lapse and that dormant integrations are fully removed after project shutdowns.

**T2. Email and account takeovers:** If a company abandons a domain once used for email addresses (e.g., `@oldcorp.com`), an attacker who re-registers it can intercept all future mail. They can impersonate the firm, send **phishing mails from the genuine domain**, or reset passwords of existing accounts [31]. Many online services rely on email for password recovery. If a former employee signed up to a cloud service with `name@oldcorp.com`, the new domain owner can use "forgot password" to gain access. Researchers warn that **trade secrets can leak** or attackers may penetrate personal accounts of ex-staff [31]. A 2025 report showed that registering domains of defunct start-ups yielded access to countless SaaS accounts. Examples included ChatGPT, Slack, Notion, Zoom, and even HR systems still tied to old email addresses [32]. Attackers viewed sensitive data such as tax forms, payslips, and applicant information [32]. The study exposed a *design problem* in single-sign-on: many providers identify users solely by email domain (the `hd` claim in Google OAuth), so a fresh Google account under the captured domain is treated as the original user [32]. Even without historical mail access, simply re-creating the address **preserves perceived identity** and unlocks accounts [32].

**T3. Threats from lingering integrations:** Beyond email, an expired domain may still be embedded in security infrastructure. Examples include **OAuth redirect URIs** or API callbacks. If such URLs point to a domain later relinquished, an attacker who captures it can control the OAuth flow. One case involved an integration using a subdomain of a now-defunct firm as its OAuth redirect; [32] after researchers bought the domain, they could masquerade as an *authenticated* organization and access data [32]. Likewise, **Single Sign On (SSO) endpoints**, API keys, or license servers may rely on the old domain. Re-using former names thus creates **bridges into previously protected areas** that the victim no longer monitors [31][32].

**T4. Drop-catching and domain speculation: Drop-catching** - automated registration of recently expired names - is not inherently criminal; an entire legitimate industry resells such domains. Fraudsters, however, also exploit it as a **business model**. With little effort they obtain domains that already **carry trust** (user familiarity, positive mail reputation, inbound links) [29]. These names are then *monetized*: directly for phishing or fraud, resold to the original owner (cybersquatting/extortion), or used for **spam/SEO** [33]. Studies show most seized domains end up in **black-hat SEO** networks - injecting links and redirects to boost dubious sites [33][34].

A headline example illustrating speculative risk occurred in 2021: Google's official Argentinian domain, `google.com.ar`, briefly lapsed and was bought for about $3 USD by a local web designer [35]. No harm ensued - he promptly returned it - but the incident shows even a tech giant can stumble, and the potential impact had an attacker acted maliciously [35].

Phase 3 therefore focuses on **keeping expired domains out of adversaries' hands**. As shown, both external users (customers) and the organization itself (through account takeover) can fall victim otherwise. For attackers, orphaned domains are attractive **attack platforms**, cloaked in legitimacy and leveraging existing trust relationships.

### *D. Phase 4: Malicious Re-registration*

Phase 4 examines the situation after a domain has been taken over by a *new owner* - often an attacker or speculator. The central question is: **How can a captured domain be exploited or monetized?**

**T1. Threats from domain speculation and trading:** Some actors register domains merely to resell them at a profit. In the harmless case, these are generic terms (e.g., `domaintrading.net`) or catchy names awaiting a buyer [36]. It becomes problematic when speculators register domains clearly linked to a company or product and then try to sell them back to the rightful owner - often at inflated prices. This practice is known as **cybersquatting**. Victims may feel extorted into repurchasing the domain to prevent abuse or protect their brand. Immediately after expiration, fraudsters can seize a domain and demand a ransom for its return [1].

**Large-scale domain parking** is another issue: studies show that a significant share of *re-registered* or never-used domains are **parked** - they host no original content, only ad links, redirects, or placeholders. According to [33], major parking providers control hundreds of thousands of such domains. Besides *trademark concerns*, parking poses *security threats*: parked domains can be repurposed for phishing or malware without notice, and it is hard for outsiders to judge whether a parked domain is benign or simply "waiting" for abuse [33].

**T2. Criminal monetization options:** Once attackers gain control of a domain - whether through typosquatting, expiration, or takeover - they acquire a highly valuable asset. **Possible revenue streams** include:

**Phishing and fraudulent sites:** As in Phase 3, a reputable domain can host convincing phishing pages. Login portals or data-theft forms seem trustworthy because the URL looks legitimate. **Fake shops** are equally common [29][37].

**Malware delivery and command-and-control:** Attackers distribute malicious files or run **Command-and-Control (C2) infrastructure** for botnets and trojans on the domain. A name absent from blacklists enjoys better initial reach. Some *Sitting Ducks* domains were used for traffic-distribution systems (TDS), spam, and **malware C2** servers [24][29].

**Spam and email scams:** A freshly registered (or hijacked) domain can host mail servers to send spam. A legacy corporate domain may still have a **good sender reputation**, reducing filter hits [1][38]. Crime groups deliberately set up mail on lapsed domains and even used them to seize social-media or SaaS accounts, as noted earlier [29].

**Leveraging residual integrations:** If the original organization still references the domain in webhooks, OAuth redirects, or API keys, the new owner can exploit that linkage. Documented cases show attackers gaining **access to enterprise data** by posing as legitimate endpoints [29][32].

**Redirects and traffic parking:** A subtler yet harmful tactic is funneling all residual traffic to ad or affiliate sites. High-traffic domains earn click revenue via automated parking platforms. While not always illegal, such redirects can tarnish brand reputation - e.g., a former corporate site suddenly points to gambling or adult content [29][33].

Overall, Phase 4 demonstrates that **attackers have many ways to profit from a seized domain**, whether financially or within larger campaigns. A domain in hostile hands becomes a **"weapon"** that slips past defenses thanks to its trusted name. For enterprises, **preventing** such takeovers must be top priority, because **damage control** afterwards is costly. Once criminals register the domain, recourse is often limited to lengthy legal action (e.g., a UDRP proceeding) or an expensive settlement - long after harm may already be done.

## IV. Conclusion and Future Work

Domains are critical security assets; a life cycle view shows distinct weaknesses before registration, during operation, after

TABLE II. SYSTEMATIC THREAT MAPPING ACROSS DOMAIN LIFE CYCLE PHASES

| Phase | Threat (ID) | Recent evidence | Primary controls |
|---|---|---|---|
| P1 | T1 Typosquatting / look-alikes | USENIX'14 [4]; NDSS'25 [1] | Defensive regs; brand watch |
| P1 | T2 Orphaned/published names | NDSS'23 [18]; Unit 42 [19] | Monitoring; claims; cleanup |
| P2 | T1 DNS misconfig | CISA [23]; Infoblox [24] | DNSSEC; CAA+CT; restrict AXFR; audits |
| P2 | T2 Subdomain takeover (dangling) | CCS'16 [6]; NSDI'24 [5] | Quarterly scans [20]; cleanup |
| P2 | T3 Registrar account compromise | IMC'22 [25]; The Guardian [26] | MFA; Registry Lock; two-party recovery |
| P3 | T1 Phishing / fraud on expired domains | S&P'22 [29]; KrebsOnSecurity [30] | Auto-renew; renewal governance; brand watch |
| P3 | T2 Email / account takeovers | IMC'24 [31]; The Hacker News [32] | Deprovisioning; retirement checklist |
| P3 | T3 Lingering integrations (OAuth / SSO / API) | IMC'24 [31]; The Hacker News [32] | Deprovisioning; OAuth/SSO audit; key revocation |
| P3 | T4 Drop-catching / speculation | TMA'22 [33]; BBC News [35] | Backorder; legal (UDRP); retain redirects |
| P4 | T1 Speculation/parking abuse | TMA'22 [33]; WIPO [34] | Monitoring; legal recourse |
| P4 | T2 Criminal monetization (phishing / C2 / spam) | Infoblox [24]; SRLabs [37] | Takedowns; blocklists; incident response |

expiration, and after re-registration.

Derivation: The conclusions synthesize the phase-wise mapping in Table II with the structured literature scan in Section II, answering RQ1-RQ2.

Implications: Domain security must be run as a continuous program across DNS configuration and registrar governance; safer defaults by registrars, registries, and CAs reduce systemic risk.

Recommendations (priority): DNSSEC on apex and critical zones; CAA; hardened registrar accounts (MFA, Registry Lock, two-party recovery); scheduled zone hygiene and takeover scans; renewal governance with deprovisioning.

Limitations: Conceptual, literature-based synthesis without new measurements; evidence focuses on 2014-2025 English-language sources; prevalence is out of scope.

Future work: (i) DNSSEC/CAA measurement; (ii) WHOIS-based re-registration/abuse analysis; (iii) registrar-security defaults; (iv) audits of SaaS/OAuth residuals during retirement.

## REFERENCES


[1] B. V. Adjibi, A. Avgeditis, M. Antonakakis, M. Bailey, and F. Monrose, "The guardians of name street: Studying the defensive registration practices of the fortune 500," in *Proceedings of the 32nd Network and Distributed System Security Symposium (NDSS 25)*, San Diego, CA, USA: Internet Society, Feb. 2025. DOI: 10.14722/ndss.2025.241202.

[2] Y. Zhang *et al.*, "Cross the zone: Toward a covert domain hijacking via shared DNS infrastructure," in *33rd USENIX Security Symposium (USENIX Security 24)*, Philadelphia, PA: USENIX Association, Aug. 2024, pp. 5751–5768, ISBN: 978-1-939133-44-1. [Online]. Available: https://www.usenix.org/conference/usenixsecurity24/presentation/zhang-yunyi-zone.

[3] S. Neupane, G. Holmes, E. Wyss, D. Davidson, and L. De Carli, "Beyond typosquatting: An in-depth look at package confusion," in *Proceedings of the 32nd USENIX Conference on Security Symposium*, ser. SEC '23, Anaheim, CA, USA: USENIX Association, 2023, ISBN: 978-1-939133-37-3.

[4] J. Szurdi *et al.*, "The long "taile" of typosquatting domain names," in *Proceedings of the 23rd USENIX Security Symposium (USENIX Security '14)*, San Diego, CA, USA: USENIX Association, Aug. 2014, pp. 191–206, ISBN: 978-1-931971-15-7. [Online]. Available: https://www.usenix.org/system/files/conference/usenixsecurity14/sec14-paper-szurdi.pdf.

[5] J. Frieß, T. Gattermayer, N. Gelernter, H. Schulmann, and M. Waidner, "Cloudy with a Chance of Cyberattacks: Dangling Resources Abuse on Cloud Platforms," in *Proceedings of the 21st USENIX Symposium on Networked Systems Design and Implementation (NSDI '24)*, USENIX Association, 2024, pp. 1977–1994, ISBN: 978-1-939133-39-7. [Online]. Available: https://www.usenix.org/conference/nsdi24/presentation/friess.

[6] D. Liu, S. Hao, and H. Wang, "All Your DNS Records Point to Us: Understanding the Security Threats of Dangling DNS Records," in *Proceedings of the 2016 ACM SIGSAC Conference on Computer and Communications Security (CCS '16)*, New York, NY, USA: Association for Computing Machinery, Oct. 2016, pp. 1414–1425, ISBN: 978-1-4503-4139-4. DOI: 10.1145/2976749.2978387. [Online]. Available: https://doi.org/10.1145/2976749.2978387.

[7] M. Squarcina, M. Tempesta, L. Veronese, S. Calzavara, and M. Maffei, "Can i take your subdomain? exploring Same-Site attacks in the modern web," in *30th USENIX Security Symposium (USENIX Security 21)*, Vancouver, B.C., Canada: USENIX Association, Aug. 2021, pp. 2917–2934, ISBN: 978-1-939133-24-3. [Online]. Available: https://www.usenix.org/system/files/sec21-squarcina.pdf.

[8] G. Schmid, "Thirty years of dns insecurity: Current issues and perspectives," *IEEE Communications Surveys & Tutorials*, vol. 23, no. 4, pp. 2429–2459, 2021. DOI: 10.1109/COMST.2021.3105741.

[9] A. Ramdas and R. Muthukrishnan, "A survey on dns security issues and mitigation techniques," in *2019 International Conference on Intelligent Computing and Control Systems (ICCS)*, 2019, pp. 781–784. DOI: 10.1109/ICCS45141.2019.9065354.

[10] A. Affinito *et al.*, "Domain name lifetimes: Baseline and threats," English, in *Proceedings of the 6th edition of the Network Traffic Measurement and Analysis Conference (TMA Conference 2022)*, International Federation for Information Processing (IFIP), Jun. 2022, ISBN: 978-3-903176-47-8. [Online]. Available: https://tma.ifip.org/2022/.

[11] G. C. M. Moura *et al.*, "Characterizing and mitigating phishing attacks at cctld scale," in *Proceedings of the 2024 on ACM SIGSAC Conference on Computer and Communications Security*, ser. CCS '24, Salt Lake City, UT, USA: Association for Computing Machinery, 2024, pp. 2147–2161, ISBN: 979-8-40-070636-3. DOI: 10.1145/3658644.3690192.

[12] M. Wang, X. Zang, J. Cao, B. Zhang, and S. Li, "Phishhunter: Detecting camouflaged idn-based phishing attacks via siamese neural network," *Computers & Security*, vol. 138, p. 103 668, Mar. 2024. DOI: 10.1016/j.cose.2023.103668. [Online]. Available: https://doi.org/10.1016/j.cose.2023.103668.

[13] Palo Alto Networks Unit 42, *The art of domain deception: Bifrost's new tactic to deceive users*, https://unit42.paloaltonetworks.com/new-linux-variant-bifrost-malware/, Retrieved: Jun. 2025, Mar. 2024.

[14] Insikt Group, "SOLARDEFLECTION: C2 Infrastructure Used by NOBELIUM in Company Brand Misuse," Recorded Future, Tech. Rep., May 2022, Retrieved: Jun. 2025. [Online]. Available: https://go.recordedfuture.com/hubfs/reports/cta-2022-0503.pdf.

[15] S. Tilborghs and G. Ferreira, "Flagging 13 million malicious domains in 1 month with newly observed domains," *Akamai Security Blog*, Sep. 2022, Retrieved: Jun. 2025. [Online]. Available: https://www.akamai.com/blog/security-research/newly-observed-domains-discovered-13-million-malicious-domains.

[16] B. Krebs, "Mastercard dns error went unnoticed for years," Retrieved: Jun. 2025, Jan. 2025. [Online]. Available: https://krebsonsecurity.com/2025/01/mastercard-dns-error-went-unnoticed-for-years/.

[17] L. Nguyen, "Byd-domain führt in deutschland zu sexspielzeug," Retrieved: Jun. 2025, Jul. 2024. [Online]. Available: https://sz.de/lux.J5FGj79Eq9c5ThRgCzKaqM.

[18] X. Li *et al.*, "Ghost domain reloaded: Vulnerable links in domain name delegation and revocation," in *Proceedings of the 2023 Network and Distributed System Security Symposium (NDSS '23)*, San Diego, CA, USA: The Internet Society, 2023. DOI: 10.14722/ndss.2023.23005.

[19] P. A. N. Unit 42, *Dangling domains: Security threats, detection and prevalence*, https://unit42.paloaltonetworks.com/dangling-domains/, Retrieved: Jun. 2025.

[20] H. N. Security, *Baddns: Open-source tool checks for subdomain takeovers*, https://www.helpnetsecurity.com/2025/02/03/baddns-open-source-tool-check-domain-subdomain-takeover/, Retrieved: Jun. 2025.

[21] R. Future, *Dnssec: What is it? how does it work?* https://www.recordedfuture.com/threat-intelligence-101/tools-and-techniques/dnssec, Retrieved: Jun. 2025.

[22] S. I. S. Center, *Quick status of the caa dns record adoption*, https://isc.sans.edu/diary/26738, Retrieved: Jun. 2025.

[23] CISA, *Dns zone transfer axfr requests may leak domain information*, https://www.cisa.gov/news-events/alerts/2015/04/13/dns-zone-transfer-axfr-requests-may-leak-domain-information, Retrieved: Jun. 2025.

[24] I. T. Intel, "DNS Predators Hijack Domains to Supply their Attack Infrastructure," Retrieved: Jun. 2025, Nov. 2024, [Online]. Available: https://blogs.infoblox.com/threat-intelligence/dns-predators-hijack-domains-to-supply-their-attack-infrastructure/.

[25] G. Akiwate *et al.*, "Retroactive identification of targeted dns infrastructure hijacking," in *Proceedings of the ACM Internet Measurement Conference (IMC '22)*, Nice, France: Association for Computing Machinery, Oct. 2022, pp. 14–32. DOI: 10.1145/3517745.3561425.

[26] A. Hern, "Lenovo website hacked and defaced by lizard squad in superfish protest," Retrieved: Jun. 2025, The Guardian, Feb. 2015, [Online]. Available: https://www.theguardian.com/technology/2015/feb/26/lenovo-website-hacked-and-defaced-by-lizard-squad-in-superfish-protest.

[27] C. Global, *Csc's 2023 domain security report finds many global 2000 companies neglect their .ai domain extensions despite surge in popularity for artificial intelligence*, https://www.cscglobal.com/service/press/many-global-2000-companies-neglect-their-ai-domains/, Retrieved: Jun. 2025.

[28] D. Chiba, H. Nakano, and T. Koide, "Domaindynamics: Advancing lifecycle-based risk assessment of domain names," *Computers & Security*, vol. 153, p. 104 366, 2025. DOI: 10.1016/j.cose.2025.104366. [Online]. Available: https://doi.org/10.1016/j.cose.2025.104366.

[29] J. So, N. Miramirkhani, M. Ferdman, and N. Nikiforakis, "Domains do change their spots: Quantifying potential abuse of residual trust," in *2022 IEEE Symposium on Security and Privacy (SP)*, 2022, pp. 2130–2144. DOI: 10.1109/SP46214.2022.9833609.

[30] B. Krebs, *That domain you forgot to renew? yeah, it's now stealing credit cards*, *KrebsOnSecurity* (blog), Retrieved: Jun. 2025, Nov. 2018. [Online]. Available: https://krebsonsecurity.com/2018/11/that-domain-you-forgot-to-renew-yeah-its-now-stealing-credit-cards/.

[31] R. Li *et al.*, "Bounce in the wild: A deep dive into email delivery failures from a large email service provider," in *Proceedings of the 2024 ACM on Internet Measurement Conference*, ser. IMC '24, Madrid, Spain: Association for Computing Machinery, 2024, pp. 659–673, ISBN: 979-8-40-070592-2. DOI: 10.1145/3646547.3688425.

[32] T. H. News, *Google oauth vulnerability exposes millions via failed startup domains*, https://thehackernews.com/2025/01/google-oauth-vulnerability-exposes.html, Retrieved: Jun. 2025.

[33] J. Zirngibl *et al.*, "Domain parking: Largely present, rarely considered!" In *Proceedings of the 6th Network Traffic Measurement and Analysis Conference (TMA '22)*, International Federation for Information Processing (IFIP), 2022, pp. 1–9. [Online]. Available: https://dl.ifip.org/db/conf/tma/tma2022/tma2022-paper26.pdf.

[34] W. I. P. O. (WIPO), *Wipo domain name report 2024: Udrp case filings remain strong*, Retrieved: Jun. 2025, 2025. [Online]. Available: https://www.wipo.int/amc/en/domains/news/2025/news_0001.html.

[35] J. Clayton, "Google argentina's domain name bought by man for £2," Retrieved: Jun. 2025, Apr. 2021, [Online]. Available: https://www.bbc.com/news/technology-56870270.

[36] Afnic Studies Team, "The global domain name market in 2023," Afnic – Association Française pour le Nommage Internet en Coopération, Tech. Rep., Jul. 2024, Retrieved: Jun. 2025. [Online]. Available: https://www.afnic.fr/wp-media/uploads/2024/07/study-afnic-the-global-domain-name-market-in-2023.pdf.

[37] M. Marx and Team, *Bogusbazaar: A criminal network of webshop fraudsters*, Security Research Labs Blog, Retrieved: Jun. 2025, May 2024. [Online]. Available: https://www.srlabs.de/blog-post/bogusbazaar.

[38] PortSwigger, *How expired web domains help criminal hackers unlock enterprise defenses*, https://portswigger.net/daily-swig/how-expired-web-domains-help-criminal-hackers-unlock-enterprise-defenses, Retrieved: Jun. 2025.

# Attesting the Trustworthiness of a Credential Issuer

Rainer Falk and Steffen Fries
Siemens AG
Foundational Technologies
Munich, Germany
e-mail: {rainer.falk | steffen.fries}@siemens.com

*Abstract*—**In some industrial environments, authentication credentials as device certificates may be issued locally. However, a locally issued credential may not be as trustworthy as credentials issued by a highly protected centralized security infrastructure. An attestation of the credential issuer can confirm evidence of its trustworthiness. Including such an attestation of the credential issuer within an issued authentication credential allows a relying party to check this information as part of credential validation. This paper proposes to embed such a cryptographically verifiable integrity attestation of a certificate issuer into issued authentication certificates.**

***Keywords–cybersecurity; attestation; credential; digital certificate; device authentication, industrial security.***

## I. INTRODUCTION

Authentication credentials, e.g., digital certificates or authentication tokens, allow a user to authenticate, i.e., to prove a claimed identity. Credentials are conventionally issued by a highly protected issuer like a Certification Authority (CA) of a Public Key Infrastructure (PKI) following well-defined operational processes, or by an Identity and Access Management (IAM) service like for instance an Open Authorization (OAuth) [1] authorization server. However, other deployment options providing local independence and increased flexibility are used in Operation Technology (OT) as well. Digital certificates or authentication tokens may, e.g., be created by engineering tools, or locally on industrial devices implementing an embedded CA (also called Alias CA), or by an edge service. The execution environments that create such credentials may therefore have different technical protections, leading to different levels of trustworthiness. Some of the used execution environments might be manipulated, e.g., if a vulnerability in the implementation can be exploited.

This paper describes how to include within an issued digital certificate a cryptographically protected attestation that confirms the integrity of the issuer's execution environment at the point in time when the digital certificate was issued. The cryptographically protected attestation confirms the actual integrity evidence of the used execution environment. Including the attestation within issued authenticators allows verifying the integrity of the execution environment in which a credential has been created. The trustworthiness of a digital certificate can therefore be determined depending on the included issuer's integrity attestation.

This approach is specifically promising if a centralized, implicitly trusted PKI is not or at least not permanently available in an operational environment. The integrity attestation of the issuing device can provide an increased level of trustworthiness for device- generated credentials, as the attestation functionality that creates the attestation can be protected at a higher level than the functionality to which the attestation relates, in particular if a hardware-based attestation implementation is used.

The remainder of the paper is structured as follows: Section II provides an overview on boundary conditions given by industrial security requirements and on technical considerations when issuing credentials. Section III introduces the concept of providing a statement of the security of the credential issuer execution environment, allowing a relying party to determine trustworthiness in the issued certificates. Section IV concludes the paper and gives an outlook towards future work.

## II. RELATED WORK

This section provides an overview of relevant related work.

### A. *Industrial Security*

Protecting Industrial Automation and Control Systems (IACS) against intentional attacks is demanded by operators to ensure a reliable operation, by industrial security standards as IEC 62443 [2], and also by regulation [3][4]. Security requirements defined by the industrial security standard IEC 62443 range from security processes during development and operation of devices and systems, personal and physical security, device security, network security, and application security, addressing the device manufacturer, the integrator, as well as the operator of the IACS. IEC 62443 specifically describes in technical requirements on system and component level, targeting four different security levels, which relate to the strength of a considered attacker. Moreover, this framework also contains specific requirements regarding authentication methods and credentials, as well as the use of cryptographic algorithms including their strength.

Industrial security is also called OT security, to distinguish it from general Information Technology (IT) security. In OT systems, actions in the digital world typically have a direct impact on the physical world. Therefore, industrial systems have different security priorities and requirements compared to common IT systems. Typically, availability and integrity of an automation system have higher priority than confidentiality. Specific requirements and side conditions of industrial automation systems like high availability, planned configuration (engineering info), scheduled maintenance windows, long life cycles, unattended operation, real-time operation, and communication, as well as safety requirements have to be considered when designing an OT security solution.

### *B. Considerations for Authentication Credentials*

Authentication credentials are used to confirm the identity of a user (human, software process, or device) towards a relying party. Examples are, besides passwords, authentication tokens, but also digital certificates. A digital certificate binds the public key of a user to the user's identity. A digital certificate can include also a certificate practice statement that provides information on the trustworthiness of the issuing process as specified in [5]. A widely used certificate format in IT and also OT applications is X.509 defined by the International Telecommunication Union (ITU-T) [6].

A digital certificate is typically issued by a CA which may be part of an engineering tool, a device management tool, a local security server, on a device, an external PKI. Alternatively, self-signed certificates directly generated on the device may be used. Standards like Trusted Computing Group's TCG specification "Device Identifier Composition Engine" (DICE) [7] and Desktop Management Task Force (DMTF) specification "Security Protocols and Data Models" (SPDM) [8] define that a device can include an internal CA for issuing device certificates, called "embedded CA" or "alias CA". It allows a device to issue a device certificate that includes information on changeable device information as its firmware version.

Certificate transparency, specified by RFC9162 [9], allows to include issued Transport Layer Security (TLS) server certificates in a public log. A digital certificate can comprise an inclusion proof to confirm that the issued certificate has in fact been included in a certificate transparency log. This supports audit of issuing CAs to detect if a CA issued certificates that were not intended by the operating organization.

### *C. Remote Attestation*

A remote attestation is a cryptographically protected data structure that can confirm security-relevant information called evidence about a device (platform attestation) or of a cryptographic key (key attestation). The Remote ATtestation procedureS (RATS) architecture [10] gives an overview on remote attestation use cases.

Meanwhile, standardization has started to adopt remote attestation also in the process of requesting certificates using different formats [11], which can be directly used in typical enrollment protocols. The defined extension allows to convey evidence and attestation results in certification requests. This in turn enhances the verification options of the issuing CA beyond the typical verification of proof-of-possession of the private key corresponding to the public key in the certification request and the proof-of-identity of the requestor to a statement about the platform properties that generated the request.

Once provided as part of a certification request, the attestation statement for the requestor may also be included in the issued certificate for later verification by the relying party.

Note that the focus of this paper is not the integrity attestation of the requestor of a certificate, but of the issuer. Both attestations can be combined, allowing to attest properties of the requester (e.g., a key attestation as statement how a keypair was generated), as well as security-relevant properties of the issuer's execution environment.

## III. Issuing Credentials Including an Issuer Attestation

A digital certificate can include a cryptographically protected attestation that confirms the issuer's integrity at the point in time when the digital certificate was issued. The cryptographically protected attestation confirms the actual integrity evidence of the execution environment of the issuer. Including the attestation within issued digital certificate allows to verify the integrity of the execution environment in which the certificate has been created. The trustworthiness of a digital certificate can therefore be determined depending on the included issuer's integrity attestation.

### *A. Digital Certificate Including Issuer Attestation*

A digital certificate binds a public key to the identifier of a subject (e.g., human user, device, process). It is signed by the issuer, e.g., a CA. It is proposed to include in addition an attestation that confirms the integrity of the issuer. For X.509 certificates, this can be easily realized by using the extension capability of certificates, allowing to include additional information by the issuer within an additional certificate extension field. This can be beneficial if it has to be assumed that the issuer itself could be manipulated, as it allows a peer validating the certificate to check the issuer's integrity status at the point in time when the digital certificate was issued.

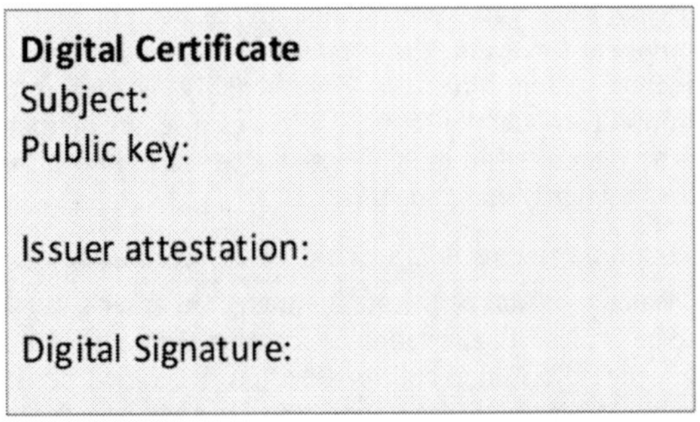


Figure 1. Digital certificate including an integrity attestation of the issuer.

Figure 1 shows the main conceptual elements of a digital certificate that includes the issuer's attestation in addition to the subject's identity and public key. This is seen as specifically useful if the issuer is a so-called embedded CA included on a device. The attestation included can be a platform attestation that allows verifying the integrity of the embedded CA issuing the digital certificate, as well as a key attestation confirming the key store type, e.g., a secure-element-based key store, of the issuer's key store, i.e., of the private key used to sign the issued digital certificate.

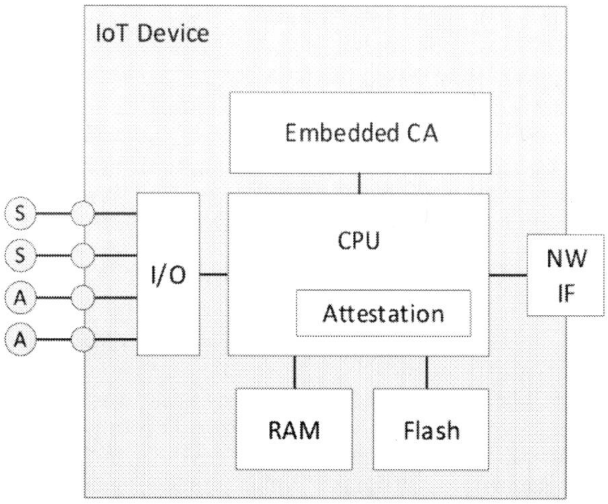


Figure 2. IoT device including an embedded CA.

Figure 2 shows an Internet of Things (IoT) device, e.g., an industrial control device, that includes an embedded CA for issuing digital device certificates. They may include identifying information, such as the device type and serial number, as well as the currently installed firmware version. The attestation included in the device certificate allows verification of the integrity status of the device, in particular of its embedded CA component.

The embedded CA on a device can be realized, e.g., by a dedicated secure element, a logically isolated enclave, or just a software component / app running on the device. This realization information may also be part of the attestation statement, which allows a relying party to make a more fine-grained decision about the issuer's trustworthiness. The device would include furthermore an Attestation Unit (AU), involving a measurement component to determine evidence in a trustworthy way (root of trust for measurements), and a component for issuing the attestation based on the determined evidence. Such attestation functionality is supported on common compute platforms, e.g., using a secure element that can be integrated in the CPU, as shown in Figure 2, or be a dedicated hardware component.

### *B. Issuing Process Adding Attestation Information*

When a digital certificate including an issuer's attestation is to be issued, an attestation concerning the certificate issuer has to be determined and included on the digital certificate. So, the determined attestation can be added to the issued certificate as part of the certificate issuing process.

The Certification Unit (CU) comprises the Registration Authority (RA) and Certification Authority (CA). It includes also the Attestation Unit (AU) with its Attestation measurement Unit (AMU) and the Attestation Signing Unit (ASU). The CU may be an internal component of a device featuring an embedded CA, as well as an external CA (e.g., in an engineering tool or standalone). The CA uses a Hardware Security Module (HSM), e.g., a crypto controller, to create the digital signature of the certificate (Cert) that is then provided to the requesting device.

In the example message sequence shown in Figure 3, the RA extends the Certificate Signing Request (CSR) received form the device with the attestation determined by AU to create the "to-be-signed certificate" data structure (tbsCert) and sends it to the CA for signing, resulting in the signed certificate including the CU's attestation. First, the device generates its key pair and the corresponding certificate signing request (CSR) and sends it to the CU's RA. The RA obtains the CU's attestation (AttCu), from the AU, and extends the received CSR accordingly by adding the CU's attestation (AttCu) as extension to the "to be signed certificate" (tbsCert). The attestation includes evidence depending on the measurements that have been obtained by the AMU. The measurements are usually collected before the attestation is built (as shown in Figure 3). However, it is also possible to determine some measurements on demand, i.e., after the attestation has been requested. The measurements may cover information on the CU's components (RA, CA), e.g., the software version and integrity information of the compute platform on which they are executed. Examples are information on whether secure boot has been active during start-up, and integrity information of the loaded and executed operating system and its components. It is also possible to attest that certain software components, as here RA and CA, are in fact executed in a isolated, protected execution environment, in particular in a specific confidential computing environment. Validating such information allows to determine whether the CU can in fact by trusted by an *external* party. Such information is complementary to manual audits that are performed for centralized PKIs, e.g., on a yearly basis. Including such information in issued certificates allows even the parties validating the certificate to check whether the CA that issued this certificate was in fact in a trustworthy state at the time when this specific certificate was issued.

Besides the included information about the platform itself, the attestation may also contain freshness information. This allows the relying party to verify that the attestation was in fact provided as part of the issuing process, i.e., that it is not stale information that has been residing on the CA for a longer time period. Freshness may be provided in different ways like:

- Application of a nonce provided by the certificate requestor. This nonce may be provided as part of the certification request as outlined in [10] and [11].
- Usage of timestamps if a real-time clock is available
- Furthermore, a hash value created deterministically from certificate content may be used, binding the attestation to the issued certificate.

Which freshness approach is best suited depends on the specific deployment scenario and the available infrastructure. In industrial automation systems, often, no (reliable) real-time clock is available.

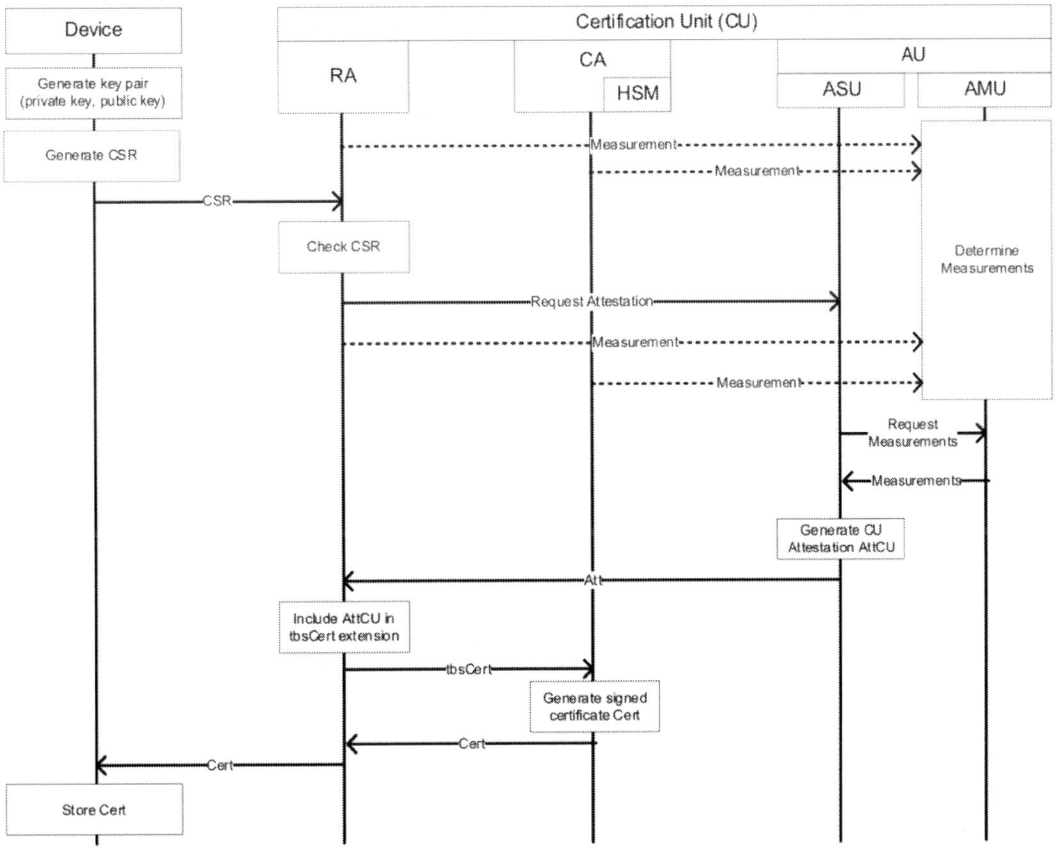


Figure 3. Including an attestation during credential issuing.

### C. *Validation a Certificate Including an Issuer Integrity Attestation*

A device can provide its digital certificate including the additional attribute (extension) including the issuer's attestation when authenticating towards a communication peer, e.g., as part of

- Transport Layer Security (TLS) authentication and key agreement.
- Network attachment to provide the device certificate as data element, e.g., towards a device/network management system.
- Application-level protocols or data exchanges utilizing digital certificates.

The relying party validates the received digital certificate following the validation rules specified in X.509 [6], which include, e.g., the verification of the subject name, validity period, certificate revocation status, but also the integrity of the digital certificate itself. Besides the digital certificate itself, also the certification path is validated. This involves the certificate of the issuing CA. For acceptance, the results have to comply with an organization's security policy. The inclusion about an attestation statement of the issuing CA in the device certificate additionally allows to match the trustworthiness of the issuing CA to an expected state necessary for processing certain data. As indicated before, this is specifically interesting for embedded CAs. Depending on the trust evaluation based on the attestation statement, a relying party may decide to, e.g.,

- limit the authoritative actions the certificate holder may perform,
- perform additional plausibility checks on data received from the device,
- provide only uncritical or non-sensitive information to the device, or
- reject interaction completely if the certificate based on the issuer information does not match the expected trustworthiness.

The attestation statement included in a digital certificate enables a more specific interaction with a device depending on its own state but also depending on the state of the issuing CA at the time of issuing the certificate.

## IV. Conclusion and Future Work

The concept described in this paper enhances authentication credentials with a statement confirming the credential issuer's platform security state. During validation, it can be matched with an operator's expectations regarding the trustworthiness of the certificate issuer. The approach allows a more fine-grained reaction based upon the attestation statement. It is planned to further evaluate the approach from a theoretical and practical perspective, including how it contributes to enhanced cyber-resilience in cyber-physical systems [12]. As part of the conceptual analysis is to analyze the expected overhead, and to evaluate relevant attack scenarios and the limitations. Further work is needed to determine how to deal with different attestation validation results. Besides rejecting a certificate, more specific reactions could be triggered, e.g., limiting associated access permissions, or planning a maintenance action as, e.g., replacement of the affected device. A prototypical implementation can support the evaluation of the performance overhead (e.g., increased size of certificates including attestation, added latency both for issuing and for validating such a certificate). Furthermore, specific scenarios of a compromised issuer can be evaluated, in particular for an issuer which security configuration is not compliant with an expected policy, and for a compromised issuer. It allows evaluating practically which scenarios can be detected based on the certificate issuer's attestation included in the certificate. The proposed approach relies on the property that the attestation functionality that creates the attestation is protected at a higher level than the credential issuing functionality to which the attestation relates. It can be evaluated in future work which attack scenarios would lead to a compromise of the attestation functionality, making the limitations of a particular attestation technology transparent. Such evaluations are the basis for deciding how well it fits a specific target environment. Which approach fits for protecting freshness of the attestation depends on the specific deployment scenario and the available infrastructure. As in industrial automation systems, often, no, or at least no reliable, real-time clock is available, other options, as outlined in Section III are alternative candidates.

Adding an issuer attestation to a certificate may be done in addition to certificate transparency [9], i.e., both approaches can be combined in a single solution. Monitoring issued certificates and the included issuer's attestation allows third parties furthermore to detect, independently of the actual usage of an issued certificate, if an issuer is not compliant anymore or if it becomes compromised. The comparison of such approaches and also of their combined usage is a further area for deeper investigation.

## References


[1] D. Hardt, "The OAuth 2.0 Authorization Framework", IETF RFC 6749, October 2012. [Online]. Available from https://datatracker.ietf.org/doc/html/rfc6749 2025.08.06

[2] IEC 62443, "Industrial Automation and Control System Security" (formerly ISA99). [Online]. Available from: http://isa99.isa.org/Documents/Forms/AllItems.aspx 2025.08.06

[3] "Regulation (EU) 2024/2847 of the European Parliament and of the Council of 23 October 2024 on horizontal cybersecurity requirements for products with digital elements and amending Regulations (EU) No 168/2013 and (EU) 2019/1020 and Directive (EU) 2020/1828 (Cyber Resilience Act), Document 32024R2847, November 2024. [Online]. Available from: http://data.europa.eu/eli/reg/2024/2847/oj 2025.08.06

[4] "Directive 2014/53/EU of the European Parliament and of the Council of 16 April 2014 on the harmonisation of the laws of the Member States relating to the making available on the market of radio equipment and repealing Directive 1999/5/EC Text with EEA relevance", 10/2023. [Online]. Available from: https://eur-lex.europa.eu/legal-content/EN/TXT/?uri=celex%3A32014L0053 2025.08.06

[5] S. Chokhani, W. Ford, R. Sabett, C. Merrill, and S. Wu, "Internet X.509 Public Key Infrastructure Certificate Policy and Certification Practices Framework", IETF RFC 3467, November 2003. [Online]. Available from https://datatracker.ietf.org/doc/html/rfc3647 2025.08.06

[6] ITU-T X.509 ISO/IEC 9594-8:2020, Rec. ITU-T X.509 (2019), Information technology – Open systems interconnection – The Directory: Public-key and attribute certificate frameworks. 2020 [Online]. Available from: https://www.itu.int/rec/T-REC-X.509-201910-I/en 2025.08.06

[7] TCG, "DICE Layering Architecture Specification". Online]. Available from: https://trustedcomputinggroup.org/resource/dice-layering-architecture/ 2025.08.06

[8] DMTF, "Security Protocols and Data Models (SPDM)", DSP0274 Version V1.3.1. [Online]. Available from: https://www.dmtf.org/sites/default/files/standards/documents/DSP0274_1.3.1.pdf 2025.08.06

[9] B. Laurie, E. Messeri, and R. Stradling, "Certificate Transparency Version 2.0", IETF RFC9162, December 2021. [Online]. Available from: https://datatracker.ietf.org/doc/rfc9162/ 2025.08.06

[10] H. Birkholz, D. Thaler, M. Richardson, Ne.Smith, and W. Pan, "Remote ATtestation procedureS (RATS) Architecture", RFC9334, December 2023. [Online]. Available from: https://datatracker.ietf.org/doc/rfc9334/ 2025.08.06

[11] M. Ounsworth, H. Tschofenig, H. Birkholz, M. Wiseman, and N. Smith, "Use of Remote Attestation with Certification Signing Requests", IETF Draft, March 2025. [Online], Available from https://datatracker.ietf.org/doc/draft-ietf-lamps-csr-attestation/ 2025.08.06

[12] R. Falk and S. Fries, "Enhanced Attack Resilience within Cyber Physical Systems", Journal on Advances in Security, vol. 16, no. 1&2, pp. 1-11, 2023. [Online]. Available from: https://www.iariajournals.org/security/sec_v16_n12_2023_paged.pdf 2025.08.06

# Selecting Cybersecurity Requirements: Effects of LLM Use and Professional Software Development Experience

Damjan Fujs, Damjan Vavpotič, Tomaž Hovelja and Marko Poženel
Faculty of Computer and Information Science
University of Ljubljana
Ljubljana, Slovenia
e-mail: {damjan.fujs | damjan.vavpotic | | tomaz.hovelja | marko.pozenel}@fri.uni-lj.si

*Abstract*—**This study investigates how access to Large Language Models (LLMs) and varying levels of professional software development experience affect the prioritization of cybersecurity requirements for web applications. Twenty-three postgraduate students participated in a research study to prioritize security requirements (SRs) using the MoSCoW method and subsequently rated their proposed solutions against multiple evaluation criteria. We divided participants into two groups (one with and the other without access to LLM support during the task). Results showed no significant differences related to LLM use, suggesting that access to LLMs did not noticeably influence how participants evaluated cybersecurity solutions. However, statistically significant differences emerged between experience groups for certain criteria, such as estimated cost to develop a feature, perceived impact on user experience, and risk assessment related to non-implementation of the proposed feature. Participants with more professional experience tended to provide higher ratings for user experience impact and lower risk estimates.**

***Keywords-security requirements engineering; experiment; prioritization; estimation.***

## I. Introduction

Software development is inherently dynamic, pushing organizations to adopt or tailor development methodologies to remain efficient and competitive [1]. Prioritization of cybersecurity requirements, especially when assisted by Large Language Models (LLMs) or shaped by prior experience, takes place within this evolving context, where structured yet adaptable decision-making is essential. Our study, therefore, addresses this crucial area. As systems grow increasingly complex and interconnected (as well as powered with Artificial Intelligence (AI) [2]), cybersecurity has become a critical concern that must be addressed early in the development lifecycle [3]. Most decisions, we can argue, are probably still made by people. In practice, it is generally accepted that longer professional experience contributes to more effective decision-making. Also, in the literature, we can find some evidence to support such claims [4]. However, some emerging ideas [5] suggest that agentic AI systems could take on decision-making roles in specific areas of cybersecurity to address evolving cyber threats.

At this stage of the study, we focus on whether there are statistically significant differences in how selected Security Requirements (from here on referred to as SR/SRs as plural) are perceived by participants who used an LLM versus those who did not. Specifically, we were interested in how participants estimated selected SRs across various evaluation criteria. This raises a broader and timely question: Can LLMs (or generative AI more broadly) begin to narrow or even erase the gap typically attributed to experience? The purpose of this paper is not to answer the question posed above, but to provide guidelines for further empirical research in the field of software engineering or software development. Additionally, we aimed to test the hypothesis on students, as they represent the next generation of software development professionals and are typically familiar with using LLMs.

Based on all the above, we hypothesize:

- **H1**: Access to a LLM has a significant effect on how participants rate their proposed SRs across the given evaluation criteria.
- **H2**: Professional experience with software development has a significant effect on how participants rate their proposed SRs across the given evaluation criteria.

Based on the proposed hypotheses, our study offers two key contributions:

- **C1**: Empirical insight into the limited impact of LLMs on cybersecurity decision-making among postgraduate students. The study provides evidence that LLM do not significantly influence how individuals prioritize or evaluate SRs.
- **C2**: Demonstration of the role of professional software development experience in prioritizing and evaluating SRs among postgraduate students. The study shows that professional software development experience significantly affects how students assess cost, user experience, and risk, highlighting the importance of practitioner expertise in shaping effective cybersecurity strategies.

The rest of the paper is organized as follows. Following this Introduction and Background section, Section II briefly highlights existing related works. Section III highlights the research methodology used. In Section IV, we present the results and discuss them briefly. In Section V we point out the limitations of our study. Finally, the conclusion and future works are presented in Section VI.

## II. Related Work

The creation of software requirements is a fundamental activity in any software project and is traditionally recognized as a labor-intensive, human-driven process [6]. Recent advances in AI, particularly the development of LLMs, have introduced new possibilities for supporting software engineering tasks such as SR engineering.

Prior research has explored various factors influencing the prioritization and evaluation of software and cybersecurity requirements, including tool support and individual expertise. Ronanki et al. [7] investigated the potential of ChatGPT to assist requirements elicitation. They found that requirements generated using ChatGPT were of higher quality than those generated by human requirements engineering experts. A similar observation was provided by Krishna et al. [6] where they found that LLMs can produce output comparable in quality to that of an entry-level software engineer when generating a software requirements specification. While general software requirements engineering has been extensively studied, particularly in terms of specification quality, tool support, and the role of human expertise, SR represents a specialized subset that introduces additional complexity. For instance, in the study of Perry et al. [8], they found that participants who had access to an AI assistant wrote significantly less secure code than those without such support, raising concerns about overconfidence in automated tools in security-critical tasks.

Moreover, previous study [9] did not find precise evidence that professional experience significantly shapes decision making in cybersecurity. In general, defining professional experience in software development is complex, as it encompasses diverse roles and learning paths, and it is similar in the field of cybersecurity. Baltes and Diehl [10] have shown that developers' self-assessments of expertise are highly context-dependent. Vadlamani and Baysal [11] suggest, that while both knowledge and experience are necessary components of software development expertise, they are not sufficient on their own, as soft skills are also important.

The above mentioned studies highlight the role of AI tools and developer expertise in software engineering, yet little is known about how these factors influence the prioritization and evaluation of security requirements. This study addresses the gap by examining the combined effects of LLM access and professional experience on cybersecurity decision-making.

## III. RESEARCH METHODOLOGY

We employed a controlled experiment [12] in our research conducted in May 2025. The participants in the experiment were postgraduate students taking a course in Advanced software development methodologies, which is offered at the University of Ljubljana, Faculty of Computer and Information Science. The course is attended by students from technical disciplines who are enrolled in various master's programs, including Computer Science and Mathematics, Computer Science, and Multimedia.

Figure 1 represents the entire research framework that consists of three main phases (e.g., Survey, Task and Analysis). The first phase involves conducting a survey. The second phase is an experiment in which participants complete a predefined task using a structured template. The final phase focuses on data analysis, including statistical testing to assess the significance between different groups and the reporting of median values.

In the first phase (*Survey*), we received informed consent from the participants in the study, explained the course of the research to them, and gave them instructions. As part of the survey, in the first phase, we collected basic data about their studies and professional experience with software engineering. The exact question for years of professional experience with software engineering was: "Excluding education, how many years have you been 'professionally' involved in software development (e.g., student work, project work, etc.)?".

In the second phase (*Task*), respondents were assigned to groups. Namely, 23 research participants were divided into two groups; one group could use any LLM for the task (experimental group, N = 12), while the other could not (control group, N = 11). Both groups had the typical time available for practicals (i.e., 2 hours, including our instructions).

We prepared a scenario and a structured template for participants to enter their decisions into. The scenario was that, as part of their work on the project (as part of the course, they were developing software to support ScrumBan [13]), they were tasked with identifying 15 SRs appropriate for enhancing the system's overall security posture. We limited participants to 15 SRs in order to establish a unified framework while reflecting the resource constraints commonly encountered in industry settings. While developing the ScrumBan web application, students gained some experience with security aspects, particularly through implementing the login user story. The implementation of the login user story required them to handle authentication mechanisms, such as enforcing password policies (e.g., minimum length of 8 characters, inclusion of various character types and numbers). Additionally, they could improve the login procedure by implementing optional enhancements, such as a password strength meter or similar features, which further encourage consideration of usability and security.

The 15 SRs, initially identified by the participants, were subsequently prioritized using the MoSCoW method [14]. The objective was to select $2X$ 'Must-have', $2X$ 'Should-have', and $2X$ 'Could-have' features from the set of 15. The remaining nine mechanisms were categorized as 'Won't have this time'. A similar prioritization approach was used in Fujs et al. [15]. The final step of the second task involved evaluating the six prioritized features using predefined criteria, as shown in Table I.

As part of this step, we aimed at gathering additional quantitative data regarding the rationale behind the participants' prioritization decisions. We used a 5-point scale ranging from 1 to 5 for each evaluation criterion. For example, in the case of Estimated Time (ET), participants were asked to assess how long it would take to implement an overdue feature, where option/value 1 corresponded to "less than 1 hour" and option/value 5 to "more than 10 hours." Intermediate options (i.e., 2, 3, and 4) were intentionally omitted to avoid over-constraining their responses and to encourage clearer distinctions in judgment. The study was conducted on-site at

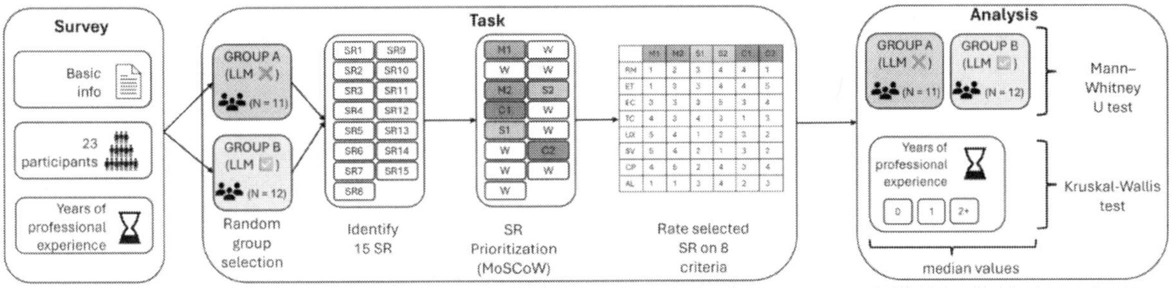


. Notes: LLM (Large Language Model), SR (Security Requirements).

Figure 1. The research framework consists of three main phases (e.g., Survey, Task and Analysis)

TABLE I. THE CRITERION WITH EIGHT ITEMS BY WHICH RESPONDENTS EVALUATED THEIR SELECTED PRIORITY SECURITY MECHANISMS.

| *ID* | *Item* | *1 - Lowest* | *5 - Highest* |
|---|---|---|---|
| 1 RM | Risk if not implemented | Minimal risk if not implemented | Critical security risk if not implemented |
| 2 ET | Estimated time | Less than 1 hour | More than 10 hours |
| 3 EC | Estimated cost | No cost, trivial to implement | High cost, external tools or experts needed |
| 4 TC | Technical complexity | Very simple, can be done without research | Very complex, requires redesign or specialized knowledge |
| 5 UX | UX impact | Almost no user impact on UX | High impact on user UX |
| 6 SV | Security value | Adds minimal security benefit | Essential for application security |
| 7 CP | Critical for production | Not needed for launch | Absolutely necessary before production release |
| 8 AL | Abuse likelihood | Very unlikely to be abused | Very likely to be abused without this feature |

the university, allowing us to control whether participants were placed in a group with access to an LLM for the task or not. Additionally, we ensured that participants could ask questions if any part of the instructions was unclear.

In the last phase (*Analysis*), we analyzed the collected data. We used appropriate non-parametric statistical tests [16] given the sample size of 23 respondents. Specifically, we employed the Mann-Whitney U test to assess whether there were statistically significant differences in prioritizations based on whether respondents did or did not use LLMs. Furthermore, respondents who were allowed to use LLMs had complete freedom to choose the LLM of their choice. Most chose the version of ChatGPT available at the time (N = 6), followed by DeepSeek (N = 2), Gemini (N = 2), Perplexity (N = 1), and Claude (N = 1). To examine differences across varying durations of professional experience, we used the Kruskal-Wallis test [16], suitable for comparing two or more groups. Based on these non-parametric tests, we then reported the Median. Based on their experience with professional software development, participants were divided into three groups: the first group included participants with zero years of experience (N = 10), the second group included participants with one year (N = 6), and the third group included participants with two or more years of experience (N = 7). This grouping was based on a qualitative judgment, as the participants were postgraduate students who were not yet formally employed. However, some had gained relevant professional software development experience through internships, freelance work, or other informal roles.

## IV. RESULTS AND DISCUSSION

Respondents selected up to six SRs using the MoSCoW prioritization method and subsequently rated each feature based on eight predefined criteria. This resulted in a total of 48 ratings per respondent (8 criteria × 6 prioritized SRs). An illustrative example of the rating form is shown in Figure 1 ("Rate selected SR on eight criteria").

The Mann-Whitney U test revealed no statistically significant differences across any of the evaluation criteria (column *item* in Figure 1). Based on these results, we conclude that access to an LLM did not significantly influence how respondents rated their proposed SRs. Therefore, Hypothesis H1 is not supported. Because we did not find significant differences, we do not report descriptive statistics (e.g., medians) for these comparisons. A possible explanation for the lack of statistically significant differences is that the LLM primarily served as a support tool for generating SRs, rather than influencing how participants evaluated their own solutions. Since the ratings were based on self-assessment, they were likely shaped more by the respondents' individual understanding, confidence, or prior knowledge than by the presence or absence of the LLM. Furthermore, given that the participants were postgraduate students with limited formal industry experience, many may have lacked the expertise to critically evaluate the quality of their proposed SRs. As a result, their assessments may have been similar across groups, regardless of LLM access.

Pavlič et al. [17] studied user story effort estimation in agile environments, comparing development teams that had assistance in generative AI tools to control teams without such support (i.e., conventional effort estimation). Contrary to our findings, they found statistically significant differences between regular and AI-assisted teams. However, it is also worth noting that in our case, it is not the same problem domain, as our respondents evaluated their own SRs (based on eight criteria), while the study participants in Pavlič et al. [17] evaluated the effort in pre-prepared user stories. Moreover, it is important to take into account the fact that in our case, the use of LLM was an option for the experimental group (i.e., we did not force the experimental group to necessarily use LLM). We intended to create a setting that approximates real-world industry conditions, where access to a given technology, such as an LLM, is available. Still, its actual use remains at the discretion of the individual.

To test hypothesis H2, we conducted a Kruskal-Wallis test [16], which revealed statistically significant differences for specific evaluation items. Table II shows five items where statistically significant differences in scores occurred for certain prioritized SRs. Items for which no statistically significant differences have been found are not shown in Table II (there were 43 such items). This result neither conclusively supports nor definitively refutes the hypothesis, as statistically significant differences were found for some items but not for most. However, it suggests that professional experience in software development may have an influence on certain evaluation criteria.

TABLE II. MEDIAN VALUES FOR ITEMS BY YEARS OF PROFESSIONAL EXPERIENCE WITH SOFTWARE DEVELOPMENT. P-VALUES INDICATE STATISTICAL SIGNIFICANCE FOR THE ITEM (ID).

| *ID* | *Years of professional experience* | *Median* | *p-value* |
|---|---|---|---|
| $S1EC$ | none (0) | 2.00 | 0.010 |
| | 1 year | 2.50 | |
| | 2+ years | 3.00 | |
| $S1UX$ | none (0) | 1.00 | 0.036 |
| | 1 year | 1.00 | |
| | 2+ years | 2.00 | |
| $S2RM$ | none (0) | 4.00 | 0.049 |
| | 1 year | 4.00 | |
| | 2+ years | 3.00 | |
| $C1RM$ | none (0) | 3.00 | 0.003 |
| | 1 year | 2.00 | |
| | 2+ years | 3.00 | |
| $C2EC$ | none (0) | 1.50 | 0.018 |
| | 1 year | 2.50 | |
| | 2+ years | 2.00 | |

The results indicate that statistically significant differences were found in the prioritization of should-have and could-have SRs, while no such differences were observed for must-have SRs. One possible explanation is that must-have SRs represent fundamental security mechanisms that are universally expected in any system (in addition, we also presented various cybersecurity mechanisms within the course, such as the OWASP (Open Worldwide Application Security Project) ASVS - Application Security Verification Standard [18]). Additionally, participants may have based their decisions on the specific characteristics of the web application they developed, leading to more consistent prioritization in this category.

C1RM achieved a p-value $< 0.01$, while S1EC, S1UX, S2RM and C2EC achieved a p-value $< 0.05$. In addition, it can also be observed that out of the eight criteria, statistically significant differences occur in three types, namely: Estimated Cost (EC), UX Impact (UX), and risk if not implemented (RM). Note that we were not interested in what actual SRs the respondents proposed, but rather in their values - that is, their assessments according to the criteria (see Table I). Among these criteria, estimated cost (EC) stands out most prominently in both S1 and C2. The results show that participants without professional experience significantly underestimated the anticipated cost of developing a proposed feature. This could be due to limited exposure to real-world development constraints such as budgeting, resource allocation, or integration complexity. In contrast, more experienced participants likely drew from hands-on experience in estimating effort and understanding hidden development costs.

In S1UX, participants with two or more years of professional experience stand out by assigning a higher median rating to the impact of the proposed feature on user experience. Similarly, in S2RM, participants with two or more years of professional experience provided slightly lower median estimates of the risk associated with not implementing the proposed feature, compared to those with no experience or only one year of experience.

## V. LIMITATIONS

While we can see some differences, it is difficult to argue about the influence of professional software development experience and the use of LLM based on these results alone. Thus, some limitations should be considered in the interpretation of these findings. First, the number of respondents is relatively small, limiting the findings' statistical power and generalizability. Second, although certain trends emerge, for instance, more experienced participants assigning higher user experience impact or lower risk estimates, these differences may also reflect individual interpretation or subjective biases rather than consistent effects of professional experience. Third, the ratings are self-reported, and participants may have relied on intuition or heuristics rather than systematic analysis, further complicating the interpretation. Therefore, while the data suggest a potential link between experience and how participants assess different aspects of cybersecurity features, these observations should be interpreted with caution.

Fourth, a potential selection bias may have occurred during group selection, as participants were assigned based on their position within the computer classroom (we counted and placed the first 11 individuals present in one group and the remaining 12 in another). This method may have unintentionally clustered individuals with similar characteristics, such as higher academic achievement, thereby affecting group comparability.

Fifth, another limitation concerns the nature and depth of LLM integration. Participants may not have fully utilized the LLM's capabilities due to time constraints, unfamiliarity with prompting, or skepticism about the tool's relevance, etc.

## VI. CONCLUSION AND FUTURE WORKS

In our research, 23 postgraduate students took part in a study aimed at prioritizing SRs using the MoSCoW method. Afterward, they evaluated their proposed solutions against several criteria. The participants were split into two groups:

one had access to LLM support during the task, while the other did not.

The study found that access to LLM did not significantly influence how participants prioritized SRs. However, professional software development experience played a notable role in shaping evaluations. Participants with more experience rated the impact on user experience higher and perceived lower risks associated with not implementing certain features. Significant differences were also observed with estimated cost, user experience, and risk assessment, highlighting the importance of domain expertise in cybersecurity decision-making.

While the current study provides valuable insights into the use of LLMs for evaluation tasks, several opportunities remain for further exploration. Future research should consider designing tasks that require deeper interaction with the model to better evaluate its potential impact for "evaluation tasks".

Future studies could incorporate external expert evaluations or peer reviews to obtain more objective assessments of solution quality. For example, it would also make sense to look at the quality - what SRs they have identified and how they have prioritized them (what mechanisms are there, which vulnerabilities do they cover, etc.). Moreover, future research could also explore how different professional roles interact with and evaluate model outputs. For instance, developers may focus on technical accuracy and implementation feasibility, project managers on delivery timelines and resource constraints, and stakeholders on strategic value and return on investment.

## ACKNOWLEDGMENTS

This work was funded by the Slovenian Research and Innovation Agency [Grant Number P2–0426]. The authors thank the participants in the research for their eager collaboration.

## REFERENCES

[1] A. Mihelič, S. Vrhovec, B. Markelj, and T. Hovelja, "Delegation-based agile secure software development approach for small and medium-sized businesses," *IEEE Access*, pp. 189 611–189 635, 2024.

[2] E. Letier and A. Van Lamsweerde, "Obstacle analysis in requirements engineering: Retrospective and emerging challenges," *IEEE Transactions on Software Engineering*, pp. 795–801, 2025.

[3] T. Jungebloud, N. H. Nguyen, D. D. Kim, and A. Zimmermann, "Model-based structural and behavioural cybersecurity risk assessment in system designs," *Computers & Security*, p. 104 543, 2025.

[5] N. Kshetri, "Transforming cybersecurity with agentic ai to combat emerging cyber threats," *Telecommunications Policy*, p. 102 976, 2025.

[6] M. Krishna, B. Gaur, A. Verma, and P. Jalote, "Using llms in software requirements specifications: An empirical evaluation," in *2024 IEEE 32nd International Requirements Engineering Conference (RE)*, IEEE, Jun. 2024, pp. 475–483.

[4] U. Franke and M. Buschle, "Experimental evidence on decision-making in availability service level agreements," *IEEE Transactions on Network and Service Management*, vol. 13, no. 1, pp. 58–70, 2015.

[7] K. Ronanki, C. Berger, and J. Horkoff, "Investigating chatgpt's potential to assist in requirements elicitation processes," in *2023 49th Euromicro Conference on Software Engineering and Advanced Applications (SEAA)*, IEEE, Sep. 2023, pp. 354–361.

[8] N. Perry, M. Srivastava, D. Kumar, and D. Boneh, "Do users write more insecure code with ai assistants?" *CCS 2023 - Proceedings of the 2023 ACM SIGSAC Conference on Computer and Communications Security*, pp. 2785–2799, Dec. 2023.

[9] M. S. Jalali, M. Siegel, and S. Madnick, "Decision-making and biases in cybersecurity capability development: Evidence from a simulation game experiment," *The Journal of Strategic Information Systems*, vol. 28, pp. 66–82, 1 Mar. 2019.

[10] S. Baltes and S. Diehl, "Towards a theory of software development expertise," in *Proceedings of the 2018 26th ACM Joint Meeting on European Software Engineering Conference and Symposium on the Foundations of Software Engineering*, ACM, Oct. 2018, pp. 187–200, ISBN: 9781450355735.

[11] S. L. Vadlamani and O. Baysal, "Studying software developer expertise and contributions in stack overflow and github," in *2020 IEEE International Conference on Software Maintenance and Evolution (ICSME)*, IEEE, Sep. 2020, pp. 312–323.

[12] V. B. Kampenes, T. Dybå, J. E. Hannay, and D. I. Sjøberg, "A systematic review of quasi-experiments in software engineering," *Information and Software Technology*, vol. 51, no. 1, pp. 71–82, 2009.

[13] M. Poženel, L. Fürst, D. Vavpotič, and T. Hovelja, "Agile effort estimation: Comparing the accuracy and efficiency of planning poker, bucket system, and affinity estimation methods," *International Journal of Software Engineering and Knowledge Engineering*, vol. 33, no. 11n12, pp. 1923–1950, 2023.

[14] E. Miranda, "Moscow rules: A quantitative exposé," in *International Conference on Agile Software Development*, Springer, 2022, pp. 19–34.

[15] D. Fujs, S. Vrhovec, and D. Vavpotič, "Balancing software and training requirements for information security," *Computers & security*, vol. 134, p. 103 467, 2023.

[16] K. Okoye and S. Hosseini, "Mann–whitney u test and kruskal–wallis h test statistics in r," in *R programming: Statistical data analysis in research*, Springer, 2024, pp. 225–246.

[17] L. Pavlič, V. Saklamaeva, and T. Beranič, "Can large-language models replace humans in agile effort estimation? lessons from a controlled experiment," *Applied Sciences*, vol. 14, no. 24, p. 12 006, 2024.

[18] S.-F. Wen and B. Katt, "A quantitative security evaluation and analysis model for web applications based on owasp application security verification standard," *Computers & Security*, vol. 135, p. 103 532, 2023.

# From Stakeholder Needs to Secure Digital Twin Services

## Critical Infrastructure Use Cases within the INTACT Framework

Ilinca-Laura Burdulea; Sonika Gogineni
Intelligent Integration Department
Fraunhofer Institute for Production Systems and Design Technology IPK
Berlin, Germany
e-mail: ilinca-laura.burdulea@ipk.fraunhofer.de, sonika.gogineni@ipk.fraunhofer.de

Stamatios Kostopoulos; Evangelos K. Markakis
Department of Electrical and Computer Engineering
Hellenic Mediterranean University
Heraklion, Greece
e-mail: s.kostopoulos@pasiphae.eu, emarkakis@hmu.gr

Kyriakos N. Manganaris; Fotis I. Lazarakis
Institute of Informatics and Telecommunications
National Centre for Scientific Research "Demokritos"
Athens, Greece
e-mail: kmangana@iit.demokritos.gr, flaz@iit.demokritos.gr

***Abstract*— Digital Twins (DTs) are a promising solution for enhancing the security and resilience of critical infrastructure. However, existing approaches rarely present systematic ways to capture stakeholder cybersecurity needs and map them to actionable functional requirements. This paper addresses that gap by presenting a user-centric methodology for deriving functional requirements for cybersecurity-focused DTs in critical infrastructures. As part of the EU-funded Integrated Software Toolbox for Secure IoT-to-Cloud Computing (INTACT) project, we apply this approach to two distinct use cases, namely a healthcare facility and a nuclear reactor facility. Stakeholder cybersecurity objectives are mapped to user stories, categorized into scenarios according to a taxonomy aligned with the Network and Information Systems (NIS2) directive, and translated into functional requirements using the INTACT reference architecture. The process highlights that cybersecurity needs are driven more by stakeholder roles than infrastructure type, enabling reuse of core DT functions across domains. By integrating user needs early in the design phase, this methodology supports systematic, replicable DT functional design with a focus on cybersecurity and human-factor risks.**

***Keywords- Digital Twin; Cybersecurity; Critical Infrastructure; Functional Requirements; NIS2 Directive.***

## I. INTRODUCTION

Critical infrastructures can be facilities, assets, systems or processes of major importance to society and whose failure or disruption would cause dramatic consequences. As these infrastructures enable the secure, reliable, and effective function of communities, ensuring their resilience and continuous functioning becomes challenging due to the increasing level of automatization and digitalization [1].

DTs are virtual images of physical systems or assets that simulate and analyse their behaviour in real-time. The virtual and physical counterparts remain synchronized through a continuous data-exchange process known as "twinning" [2]. Robotics, data-driven modelling, cloud computing, the Internet of Things (IoT), and Artificial Intelligence (AI) are few of the technologies that enable the realization of DTs [3].

By creating DTs of their IT infrastructure, networks, and security systems, organizations can simulate cyber-attacks, analyse vulnerabilities, and test response plans in a controlled virtual environment before deployment in the actual system [4]. Since DTs enable continuous monitoring, threat detection, and risk mitigation, they can exploit real-time cyber intelligence and thus contribute to stronger and more resilient critical infrastructure systems [5][6].

However, effective implementation requires stakeholders to be considered from the concept development phase. Their roles and objectives should inform the design of DT functions to create relevant and user-centered services. While the "user focus" dimension in DT application dimensions, as defined by Uhlenkamp et al. [7], only distinguishes between single-user and multi-user approaches, accounting for a broader range of stakeholder perspectives can significantly enhance value creation within DT ecosystems [8].

Although cybersecurity is acknowledged in recent DT architectural frameworks, its functional implementation remains inconsistent. Despite rich literature on DT development, a comprehensive, user-centric methodology tailored to cybersecurity is yet to be established. Systematic reviews have identified key gaps, including the lack of standardized security modelling, the absence of integrated multi-domain frameworks, and the need for more proactive and adaptive security models [9][10].

To address these gaps, we propose a functional, user-centric modelling methodology for DTs with a strong focus on cybersecurity in critical infrastructure contexts. This methodology maps stakeholder needs and objectives concerning cybersecurity to user stories, from which system requirements are derived. We demonstrate its applicability using two distinct use cases, namely a healthcare facility and a nuclear reactor facility, to highlight the potential for creating a unified, cross-domain cybersecurity framework for DTs in critical infrastructures. Embedding security by design, this approach makes cybersecurity more accessible, systematic, and scalable, ultimately contributing to enhanced protection and resilience of critical infrastructure systems.

The rest of this paper is organized as follows: Section II reviews related work and outlines the research gap. Section III presents the broader context of the INTACT project. Section IV introduces the proposed methodology for mapping stakeholder cybersecurity needs into functional requirements. Section V demonstrates the application of this methodology to two critical infrastructure use cases, and Section VI concludes with a discussion and outlook.

## II. Related Work

DTs are widely recognized as a transformative technology for managing complex systems, as they combine real-time data, simulations, visualizations, and predictions to enable system optimization and informed decisions. In the context of critical infrastructures, DTs are a relevant solution for improving operational efficiency, resilience, and overall security, since they address security, trust, and privacy challenges in these domains [11]. For example, in the healthcare sector, DTs can serve as a conceptual framework for analysing data-driven practices and improving both operational and clinical processes [12]. Cybersecurity applications include vulnerability detection [13] and securing Wireless Body Area Networks (WBAN) [14]. In the nuclear domain, DTs are still in the early stage of adoption but are gradually being implemented across the full lifecycle: from design to operation, maintenance and decommissioning [15]. However, cybersecurity applications remain limited, mostly focused on testbeds for physical protection systems [16] or high-level functional and risk assessments [17].

Although cybersecurity is acknowledged in most recent DT reference architectures, its implementation varies across frameworks and lacks methodological consistency:

*1) Layered Security:* Frameworks such as the Industrial Internet Reference Architecture (IIRA) [18] and IoT Reference Architecture (IoT RA) [19] treat cybersecurity as a cross-cutting concern, providing granular security mechanisms applied at each architectural layer. Eckhart and Ekelhart [20] exemplify this by implementing state replication to detect anomalies at each architectural layer.

*2) Security Analytics as an External Function:* In frameworks such as the DT2SA [21], DTs function as data aggregators and processors, while security analytics is applied sequentially rather than being inherently integrated. Similarly, Coppolino et al. [22] use external applications to process and analyse twin data, treating cybersecurity as an add-on rather than an integrated feature.

*3) Security by Design:* This type of approach embeds cybersecurity from the initial design phase, rather than adding it through external applications [23]. For example, De Benedictis et al. [24] extend the general 5D model proposed by Tao et al. [25] with a dedicated cross-component security layer, ensuring foundational protection.

Despite the diversity in approaches, a systematic methodology for developing cybersecurity-relevant system functions based on stakeholder needs is still missing. A systematic mapping study [9] highlights key gaps:

- *Lack of Standardized Security Modelling*: out of 261 DT papers analysed, only 17 explicitly considered security as a quality attribute, despite its relevance under the ISO25010 standard of software product quality.
- *Absence of Multi-Domain Flexibility*: Most solutions are domain-specific, with 86% of analysed proposals being designed for individual sectors. This limits scalability of security mechanisms across infrastructures.
- *Reactive Rather than Proactive Security*: Many existing frameworks adopt a reactive approach on cybersecurity, where security measures are applied post hoc, on top of the existing layers, through external analytics or monitoring tools.

As defined by Uhlenkamp et al. [7], the "user focus" dimension in DTs distinguishes between single- and multi-user frameworks. However, recent research shows that DTs generate significantly more value when designed to support multiple stakeholders with different objectives, responsibilities, and decision-making capabilities [8]. Since stakeholder actions and decisions are interdependent and affect the DT ecosystem evolution [26], supporting these varied needs within a single DT environment improves situational awareness, enhances decision-making, and improves alignment across organizational layers. This is particularly important in cybersecurity, where roles such as IT staff, compliance officers, risk managers, and engineers require coordinated access and responsibilities.

Given that human factors such as lack of awareness are perceived as one of the most dangerous issues in cybersecurity [27], directly mapping stakeholder needs and actions to DT system requirements helps anticipate and mitigate these risks by ensuring the system supports the users effectively and contributes to adequate cybersecurity governance.

Few studies examine stakeholder involvement in DT design methodologies. For example, De Benedictis et al. [24] mention a Human-Machine Interface (HMI) suitable for various user types but does not explain how stakeholder needs are translated into system design. A conceptually closer approach is presented in [8], which explores stakeholders and their requirements for DTs; however, its stakeholder categories are general for Industry 4.0 [28] and differ from the cybersecurity focus central to our methodology. A cybersecurity-oriented DT for critical infrastructures has been proposed by Masi et al. [23] using reference models and layered viewpoints, however stakeholder concerns are handled only abstractly through these views.

Our work builds on the general methodology proposed by Lünnemann et al. [29] which maps user stories to functional requirements, by introducing a cybersecurity-specific focus and a way to categorize scenarios accordingly. In doing so, we address an important methodological gap: how to systematically map stakeholder needs into functional requirements for DTs specifically designed for cybersecurity. Our approach provides a user-centric methodology that operationalizes Security by Design at the functional level.

## III. INTACT Vision and Reference Architecture

The INTACT reference architecture is a modular, service-based DT framework designed for cybersecurity in IoT-to-Cloud infrastructures. It enables diverse stakeholders to secure and manage networked systems by supporting key objectives, such as device trustworthiness, information security, privacy, governance, employee training, and the simulation and evaluation of cybersecurity scenarios.

The architecture is structured across three layers: physical infrastructure, DT infrastructure, and DT services. The DT infrastructure replicates the physical system's behaviour, data, and control logic using twinning agents, while the DT services layer hosts cybersecurity capabilities provided by a dedicated toolbox. This toolbox may be deployed within the DT environment or accessed remotely (e.g., via a data space), depending on the use case. It offers interoperable services and a user dashboard for selecting, orchestrating, and monitoring security operations. These capabilities form the basis of six key functional requirement categories that support cybersecurity in DT, as illustrated in Figure 1:

*1) Predictive Threat Intelligence Engine:* processes data from automated inspection engines, twinning agents, and simulations to forecast threats and recommend mitigation;

*2) Automated Software and Firmware Inspection Engine:* uses static/dynamic analysis and AI-driven probes to identify vulnerabilities in system binaries and data flows;

*3) Cybersecurity Orchestration Layer:* coordinates responses across systems, integrating DT insights with live networks via interfaces and open connectors;

*4) Dashboard and Assistance Layer:* provides control over service deployment, integrates explainable AI outputs, and gives access to cybersecurity awareness training;

*5) Digital and Broker Interfaces:* enable communication with external data spaces, remote services, and interoperability with other DT environments;

*6) User Interfaces:* support stakeholder-specific views and interactions, including a virtual assistant.

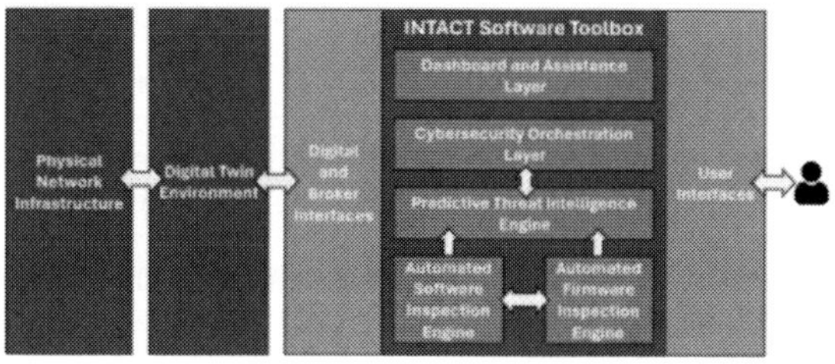


Figure 1. INTACT reference architecture, including the six functional cybersecurity elements previously mentioned.

Together, these functional components enable flexible, proactive cybersecurity services within DT ecosystems, designed to scale across domains while embedding cybersecurity at the architectural level.

## IV. Methodology

The presented methodology is a structured, stakeholder-driven approach to deriving functional requirements for cybersecurity-specific DTs in critical infrastructures based on user stories. While inspired by the modular development sequence proposed by Lünnemann et al. [29], which extends Cockburn's functional requirements-based system design [30] with data flow considerations [31], this work follows a distinct trajectory focused on cybersecurity needs. Unlike Lünnemann et al. [29], who modularize scenarios to define DT sub-functions, our methodology uses a cybersecurity-specific taxonomy to categorize them. This approach keeps security concerns explicit throughout the process and aligns functional requirements with stakeholder cybersecurity objectives, rather than simply identifying necessary sub-functions. In this way, we maintain a continuous emphasis on security priorities and their traceability into the DT architecture.

Stakeholder input is first captured through user stories, which are grouped into operational scenarios. These scenarios are then categorized using a cybersecurity-specific taxonomy and ranked based on criteria such as potential impact and likelihood of occurrence. Finally, the categorized scenarios are mapped to functional requirements based on the INTACT reference architecture. This results in a complete and traceable path from user needs to system capabilities in the context of cybersecurity, maintaining conceptual clarity while being adaptable across critical infrastructure domains. The methodology lays a foundation for further development: identified functional requirements can be complemented by parallel data flow analysis [31] to derive the necessary system architecture, which can be iteratively refined as more sub-functions of the DT are developed.

### A. Stakeholder Identification and User Story Definition

The process begins by identifying stakeholders whose responsibilities intersect with cybersecurity concerns in both use cases. Stakeholder selection is based on operational duties, regulatory obligations, and interaction with the DT environment. User stories are then derived through interviews with relevant personnel, including operational staff, cybersecurity managers, and supporting roles. All stories follow a standardized format to ensure consistency and documentation: *"As a <role>, I would like to <function>, so that <value>".*

### B. Scenario Definition and Cybersecurity Taxonomy

User stories are clustered into scenarios that describe the system functions required to achieve the expected added value in individual, operational steps. While Lünnemann et al. [29] use standardized dimensions to describe scenarios, this work introduces a tailored cybersecurity-specific taxonomy for identifying corresponding functional requirements. The taxonomy is derived from Article 21 of the NIS2 Directive [32], the EU-wide regulatory framework governing cybersecurity risk management in critical infrastructures. Based on this, we define three categories:

*1) Compliance and Governance:* describing formal policies, governance structures, and audit mechanisms required to meet legal and regulatory obligations;

*2) Operational Security:* covering everyday security processes that maintain a protective posture;

*3) Threat Modelling and Intelligence:* referring to the identification and analysis of potential risks and vulnerabilities.

Each of these categories includes four subcategories, shown in Table I, which provide a more granular structure for classifying and prioritizing scenarios. While NIS2 does not prescribe a fixed taxonomy, this interpretation reflects the coverage of its risk management requirements in a way that is both actionable and adaptable to the context of DT development. It is important to note that several user stories naturally span multiple subcategories (or even categories), given the inherent overlap between compliance, operational practice, and risk-analysis in real-world cybersecurity settings. Therefore, the taxonomy shown in Table I supports flexible mapping that preserves the integrity of stakeholder input while enabling structured prioritization based on both operational relevance and regulatory alignment.

TABLE I. CYBERSECURITY-FOCUSED TAXONOMY FOR DEFINING SCENARIOS

| Category | Subcategory | Description |
|---|---|---|
| Compliance and Governance | Regulatory Compliance | Ensuring adherence to legal frameworks and industry-specific mandates. |
| | Policy Monitoring | Monitoring enforcement of security policies and detecting compliance violations. |
| | Access Governance | Managing identity, authentication, and access control to secure systems and data. |
| | Organizational Awareness | Providing security insights and reports to stakeholders and decision-makers. |
| Operational Security | Network Monitoring | Observing traffic, performance, and behavior of systems for anomalies. |
| | Incident Management | Identifying security events and coordinating timely, effective incident responses. |
| | Security Configuration | Testing, configuring, and validating defensive setups and security policies. |
| | Device and Data Protection | Securing endpoints, sensitive data, and communications from compromise. |
| | Continuity and Recovery | Ensuring operational resilience through backups, recovery strategies, and testing. |
| Threat Modeling and Intelligence | Vulnerability Analysis | Discovering weaknesses in systems or configurations that attackers might exploit. |
| | Threat Simulation | Simulating potential attacks and modeling future threat scenarios based on current data. |
| | Trust and Behaviour Analysis | Analyzing user/device behavior and trustworthiness to detect anomalies and malicious intent. |
| | Risk Assessment | Evaluating the likelihood and impact of threats to prioritize mitigation strategies. |

### C. Importance Ranking and Mapping to Functional Requirements

Once scenarios are categorized, they are ranked based on their relevance to the specific use case and potential impact on security posture. This prioritization helps focus system development on high-value or high-risk areas first.

Instead of modularizing scenarios into detailed system modules, functional requirements are derived from the scenario content at the capability level. These requirements describe the system capabilities required to address stakeholder needs as reflected in the scenarios, while maintaining flexibility and abstraction.

The INTACT toolbox provides one potential reference architecture, consisting of the following functional components: predictive threat intelligence engine, automated software and firmware inspection engine, cybersecurity orchestration layer, dashboard and assistance layer, digital and broker interfaces, and user interfaces. Nevertheless, the functional requirements themselves can be adapted to alternative architectures. The upstream methodology (spanning user stories, taxonomy, and scenario categorization) remains generalizable and is compatible with future cybersecurity-focused system applications and architectures.

## V. APPLICATION TO CRITICAL INFRASTRUCTURE USE CASES

The proposed methodology is applied to two critical infrastructure scenarios: a healthcare facility and a nuclear reactor facility. For each, we first provide an overview of selected key stakeholders, their responsibilities, and main cybersecurity concerns. A mapping example is presented, connecting selected user stories of a specific stakeholder to categorized scenarios, and linking them to functional requirements within the DT environment according to the INTACT reference architecture.

### A. Healthcare Facility Use Case

*1) Stakeholders:* Out of six identified stakeholders, we describe here three primary ones selected for their central role in hospital operation and security. *The Information, Communications, and Technology (ICT) Administrator* ensures network security by monitoring performance, detecting anomalies, simulating network changes, and enforcing access controls. *The Cybersecurity Engineer* focuses on threat detection and mitigation by analyzing security logs, predicting attack vectors, simulating incident responses, and integrating threat intelligence. *The Biomedical Operator* supports safe device operation by reporting system issues, responding to device alerts, and maintaining secure authentication. These roles collaborate closely to secure both IT systems and clinical devices.

*2) Cybersecurity Concerns:* These include compromise of medical IoT devices (e.g., imaging systems or wearables) that can falsify readings or disrupt patient care, breaches of patient data leading to security violations, ransomware locking critical hospital systems and records, phishing or social engineering enabling credential theft and malware deployment, and data exfiltration through insufficient monitoring or access controls.

*3) Example Mapping:* Table II presents a selected mapping of the three highest-priority user stories for the *Biomedical Operator*, categorized and linked to DT functional requirements. Each follows the standardized format introduced earlier. While some user stories resulted in multiple functional requirements, a single example for each user story is listed for conciseness. In total, 25 user stories were derived across the six identified stakeholders.

TABLE II. BIOMEDICAL OPERATOR EXAMPLE MAPPING (HEALTHCARE FACILITY USE CASE)

| User story *(As a Biomedical Operator…)* | Category | Subcategory | Functional Requirement |
|---|---|---|---|
| I want to be alerted if a medical device is compromised by a cyberattack so that I can take appropriate action. | Operational Security | Device and Data Protection | Issue real-time alerts when connected medical devices show signs of compromise or abnormal behavior (Cybersecurity Orchestration Layer). |
| I want to authenticate fast and securely in the IT systems of the hospital so that I am efficient in my patient care. | Compliance and Governance | Access Governance | Support secure and rapid user authentication compatible with badges or biometric access systems (User Interface). |
| I want to report suspicious IT behavior easily so that I can contribute to the hospital's security. | Compliance and Governance | Organizational Awareness | Provide a streamlined user interface for staff to report suspicious IT behavior to the cybersecurity team (User Interface). |

## B. Nuclear Reactor Facility Use Case

*1) Stakeholders:* Out of five identified stakeholders, we describe here three primary ones selected for their central role in the operation and security of the infrastructure. *The Operational Technology (OT) System Engineer* ensures system integrity by monitoring components, detecting anomalies, running failure tests, and tracking configuration changes. *The IT Administrator* oversees IT/OT integration, manages tools, checks access logs, handles alerts, and performs cross-domain tests. *The Cybersecurity Analyst* detects and mitigates threats by correlating logs, simulating incidents, prioritizing defenses, and enforcing zero-trust policies. These stakeholders work in close coordination, with *the OT System Engineer* providing operational insights to *the IT Administrator* for secure system integration, while both collaborate with *the Cybersecurity Analyst* to ensure comprehensive threat detection and response across IT and OT domains.

*2) Cybersecurity Concerns:* These include false data injection that can mislead network stakeholders or automated safety operations, misconfigurations of components such as remote access protocols, firewalls or switches that create vulnerabilities, malware or ransomware propagation that disrupts operations or damages critical assets, and Distributed Denial-of-Service (DDoS) attacks that overload safety-related systems.

*3) Example Mapping:* Table III presents a selected mapping of the four highest-priority *IT Administrator* user stories, categorized, and linked to their corresponding DT functional requirements. Across the five identified stakeholders, a total of 18 user stories were derived.

TABLE III. IT ADMINISTRATOR EXAMPLE MAPPING (NUCLEAR REACTOR FACILITY USE CASE)

| User story *(As an IT Administrator…)* | Category | Subcategory | Functional Requirement |
|---|---|---|---|
| I want to integrate IT/OT network monitoring tools into a unified dashboard so that I can assess system security and performance. | Operational Security | Network Monitoring | Provide a real-time dashboard that aggregates and visualizes IT/OT network monitoring data (Dashboard and Assistance Layer). |
| I want to monitor access logs across both IT and OT systems so that I can detect unusual access attempts. | Compliance and Governance | Access Governance | Collect and correlate IT and OT access logs to detect suspicious or unauthorized activity (Cybersecurity Orchestration Layer). |
| I want to receive real-time alerts for anomalies in IT-OT data flows so that I can react quickly to threats. | Operational Security | Incident Management | Identify anomalies in IT-OT data flows and generate real-time alerts for potential threats (Predictive Threat Intelligence Engine). |
| I want to simulate IT-originating cyberattacks into OT systems so that I can evaluate response strategies. | Threat Modeling and Intelligence | Threat Simulation | Enable simulation of IT-based cyberattacks propagating into OT systems for response evaluation (Digital and Broker Interfaces). |

The two use cases demonstrate the applicability of the proposed methodology across distinct critical infrastructures.

# VI. CONCLUSION AND FUTURE WORK

This paper presented a methodology for systematically deriving functional requirements for cybersecurity-focused DTs by mapping stakeholder-derived user stories, categorized according to a cybersecurity-specific scenario taxonomy, to the INTACT reference architecture. The methodology was investigated through its application to two use cases in critical infrastructure (a healthcare facility and a nuclear reactor facility), demonstrating that the approach is valid and that the functional requirements derived are primarily informed by stakeholder needs rather than infrastructure type. By creating a mapping between stakeholder objectives and functional requirements, the methodology directly addresses human-factor risks, which are a recognized key vulnerability in cybersecurity.

However, it remains unclear whether the identified functional requirements fully reflect stakeholder objectives, as no downstream validation step is included. The current methodology models user needs upstream in a consistent and replicable way, but a validation procedure to confirm alignment during or after the implementation is still planned as future work. Another consideration is that outcomes may vary depending on the constraints of the chosen reference architecture. Interestingly, despite different stakeholders, functional requirements were also shared across use cases, suggesting general applicability of the taxonomy, though some overlapping categories created modeling challenges.

This methodology offers a strong foundation for further development. Future steps will include supplementing this approach with data flow analysis to iteratively refine the sub-functions of the architecture by capturing additional details (e.g., data sources and sinks, potential data bottlenecks). This will support both the implementation and later validation of core functions against stakeholder needs.

## ACKNOWLEDGMENT

The cybersecurity taxonomy used in this methodology was developed with valuable input from discussions with Bernhard Garn (SBA Research, Viena, Austria).

## REFERENCES

[1] G. Smith, J. Brown, and A. Johnson, "Critical infrastructure protection: Requirements and challenges for the 21st century," International Journal of Critical Infrastructure Protection, vol. 8, no. 4, pp. 53-66, 2015.

[2] M. D. Nord, "Digital twin: Mitigating unpredictable, undesirable emergent behavior in complex systems," in Transdisciplinary Perspectives on Complex Systems, F.-J. Kahlen, S. Flumerfelt, and A. Alves, Eds. Cham: Springer, pp. 85-113, 2017.

[3] Y. Jiang, S. Yin, K. Li, H. Luo, and O. Kaynak, "Industrial applications of digital twins," Philos. Trans. R. Soc. A Math. Phys. Eng. Sci, vol. 379, no. 2194, p. 20200360, 2021.

[4] A. Rasheed, O. San, and T. Kvamsdal, "Digital twin: Values, challenges and enablers from a modeling perspective," IEEE Access, vol. 8, pp. 21980-22012, 2020.

[5] S. A. Varghese, A. D. Ghadim, A. Balador, Z. Alimadadi, and P. Papadimitratos, "Digital Twin-Based Intrusion Detection for Industrial Control Systems," in Proc. IEEE Int. Conf. Pervasive Comput. Commun. Workshops (PerCom Workshops), pp. 611-617, 2022.

[6] M. H. Homaei, O. Mogollón Gutiérrez, J. C. Sancho Núñez, and M. Ávila, "A review of digital twins and their application in cybersecurity based on artificial intelligence," Artif. Intell. Rev., vol. 57, no. 8, pp. 201-265, 2024.

[7] J.-F. Uhlenkamp, K. Hribernik, S. Wellsandt, and K.-D. Thoben, "Digital Twin Applications: A First Systemization of Their Dimensions," in Proc. 2019 IEEE Int. Conf. Eng., Technol. Innov. (ICE/ITMC), pp. 1-8, 2019.

[8] R. Liyanage, N. Tripathi, T. Päivärinta, and Y. Xu, "Digital twin ecosystems: Potential stakeholders and their requirements," in Software Business, J. Springer and J. Manner, vol. 463, pp. 19-34, 2022.

[9] E. Ferko, A. Bucaioni, and M. Behnam, "Architecting digital twins," IEEE Access, vol. 10, pp. 50335-50350, 2022.

[10] D. M. Botín-Sanabria et al., "Digital twin technology challenges and applications: A comprehensive review," Remote Sens., vol. 14, no. 6, Art. no. 1335, 2022.

[11] G. Lampropoulos, X. Larrucea, and R. Colomo-Palacios, "Digital twins in critical infrastructure," Information, vol. 15, no. 8, Art. no. 454, 2024.

[12] R. Zhang, F. Wang, J. Cai, and Y. Wang, "Digital twin and its applications: A survey," Int. J. Adv. Manuf. Technol., vol. 123, no. 3, pp. 4123–4136, 2022.

[13] J. Zhang et al., "Cyber resilience in healthcare digital twin on lung cancer," IEEE Access, vol. 8, pp. 201900-201913, 2020.

[14] V. Rajasekar and K. Sathya, "Healthcare cyberspace: medical cyber physical system in digital twin," in Digital Twin Technologies for Healthcare 4.0, Chapter 7, pp. 113-130, 2023.

[15] H. Mengyan, X. Zhang, C. Peng, Y. Zhang, and J. Yang, "Current status of digital twin architecture and application in nuclear energy field," Annals of Nuclear Energy, vol. 202, p. 110491, 2024.

[16] Y. Guo, A. Yan, and J. Wang, "Cyber Security Risk Analysis of Physical Protection Systems of Nuclear Power Plants and Research on the Cyber Security Test Platform Using Digital Twin Technology," in 2021 International Conference on Power System Technology (POWERCON), pp. 1889-1892, 2021.

[17] X. Lou, Y. Guo, Y. Gao, K. Waedt, and M. Parekh, "An Idea of Using Digital Twin to Perform the Functional Safety and Cybersecurity Analysis," in GI-Jahrestagung, pp. 283-294, 2019.

[18] The Industrial Internet of Things: Reference Architecture, Version 1.9, Industrial Internet Consortium, 2019.

[19] ISO/IEC 30141:2024 - Internet of Things (IoT) - Reference architecture, International Organization for Standardization and International Electrotechnical Commission, Geneva, Switzerland, 2024.

[20] M. Eckhart and A. Ekelhart, "A Specification-based State Replication Approach for Digital Twins," in Proc. 2018 Workshop on Cyber-Physical Systems Security and PrivaCy (CPS-SPC '18), Toronto, ON, Canada, pp. 36-47, 2018.

[21] A. Alsarhan and M. Al-Jarrah, "Digital-twin-based security analytics for the Internet of Things," Information, vol. 14, no. 2, p. 95, 2023.

[22] L. Coppolino, R. Nardone, A. Petruolo, and L. Romano, "Building cyber-resilient smart grids with digital twins and data spaces," Applied Sciences, vol. 13, no. 24, p. 13060, 2023.

[23] M. Masi, G. P. Sellitto, H. Aranha, and T. Pavleska, "Securing critical infrastructures with a cybersecurity digital twin," Software Syst. Model., vol. 22, no. 2, pp. 1-19, 2023.

[24] A. De Benedictis, N. Mazzocca, A. Somma, and C. Strigaro, "Digital Twins in Healthcare: An Architectural Proposal and Its Application in a Social Distancing Case Study," IEEE J. Biomed. Health Inform., vol. 27, no. 10, pp. 5143-5154, 2023.

[25] F. Tao et al., "Five-dimension digital twin model and its ten applications," Comput. Integr. Manuf. Syst., vol. 25, no. 1, pp. 1-18, 2019.

[26] M. Tsujimoto, Y. Kajikawa, J. Tomita, and Y. Matsumoto, "A review of the ecosystem concept - Towards coherent ecosystem design," Technol. Forecast. Soc. Change, vol. 136, pp. 49-58, 2018.

[27] A. Hussain, A. Mohamed, and S. Razali, "A Review on Cybersecurity: Challenges & Emerging Threats," in Proc. 3rd Int. Conf. Networking, Information Systems & Security (NISS), Art. no. 28, pp. 1-7, 2020.

[28] H. Lasi, P. Fettke, H.-G. Kemper, T. Feld, and M. Hoffmann, "Industry 4.0," Bus. Inf. Syst. Eng., vol. 6, pp. 239-242, 2014.

[29] P. Lünnemann, K. Lindow, and L. Goßlau, "Implementing digital twins in existing infrastructures," Forsch. Ingenieurwes., vol. 87, pp. 1-9, 2023.

[30] A. Cockburn, Writing Effective Use Cases, 16th ed. Boston: Addison-Wesley, 2006.

[31] A. Seegrün, P. Lünnemann, and K. Lindow, "Methodische Analyse bestehender Wertschöpfungssysteme zur Integration Digitaler Zwillinge [Methodical Analysis of Existing Value Creation Systems for the Integration of Digital Twins]," ProduktDatenJournal, no. 2, pp. 42-47, 2021.

[32] European Parliament and Council, "Directive (EU) 2022/2555 on high common cybersecurity level (NIS 2)," Off. J. Eur. Union, vol. L 333, pp. 80-152, 2023.

# Proposal and Implementation of a Security Enhancement Method using Route Hopping MTD for Mesh Networks

Yuto Ikeda
Graduate School and Faculty of Information Science and Electrical Engineering, Kyushu University
Fukuoka, Japan
e-mail: ikeda.yuto.181@s.kyushu-u.ac.jp

Hiroshi Koide
Research Institute for Information Technology, Kyushu University
Fukuoka, Japan
e-mail: koide@cc.kyushu-u.ac.jp

***Abstract*—Mesh networking has recently garnered significant attention in the Internet of Things (IoT) domain. In a mesh network, the nodes are interconnected in a mesh topology; compared to the star topology traditionally employed in many IoT systems, it offers greater fault tolerance through dynamic routing and an extended communication range. Although these advantages have led to the widespread adoption of mesh networks, the practice of forwarding packets across heterogeneous devices introduces notable security vulnerabilities. This paper presents the design and implementation of an IoT communication scheme that integrates Moving Target Defense (MTD) mechanisms—previously studied mainly in IP networks—into mesh-based IoT environments. The implemented scheme improves security by extending the conventional Ad hoc On-demand Distance Vector (AODV) protocol and applying MTD to route selection. In this method, multiple candidate paths are discovered during route exploration and one route is randomly selected for each packet when forwarding packets. The scheme mitigates man-in-the-middle and Denial-of-Service (DoS) attacks originating from a single compromised node by dynamically selecting and rotating among multiple routing paths. To evaluate performance, we implemented the proposed method in Python for Raspberry Pi and we measure and compare the processing time of the proposed scheme with that of ordinary simple Ad hoc On-demand Distance Vector (AODV) routing.**

***Keywords-IoT; Mesh Network; Moving Target Defense; AODV.***

## I. Introduction

### A. Purpose

In this paper, we implement a new security method that combines *route hopping*—a form of Moving Target Defense (MTD)—with the Ad hoc On-demand Distance Vector (AODV) routing protocol in IoT mesh networks. In conventional mesh networks, a route is used continuously once it has been discovered, which creates security concerns. This paper addresses that issue by applying a Moving Target Defense approach to improve security. Our specific contributions are summarized below:

1) Route-Hopping MTD Design: We implement the scheme that randomly assigns the packet-forwarding path per packet in an AODV-based mesh, adding some lightweight extensions.
2) Prototype Implementation and Evaluation: We implemented the Algorithm in Python on Raspberry Pi nodes with Bluetooth Low Energy (BLE). We implemented a virtual-mesh network using Raspberry Pi's BLE, and tested the Route-Hopping MTD Algorithm. The evaluation shows that security can be improved with only minimal overhead. As the first case of experimentation in a real environment, we obtained results consistent with previous simulation-based studies, thereby confirming the feasibility of the approach in practice. In particular, when conducting an experiment with five nodes and two candidate routes, the overhead was limited to only an additional 1 ms in packet forwarding time. These findings indicate that distributing traffic across multiple routes can realistically improve security without imposing significant performance overhead.

### B. Motivation

In recent years, IoT devices have proliferated explosively, and by connecting a wide variety of equipment to a network, they now provide an equally diverse range of functions. These functions require a communication network, yet supporting large numbers of devices over wide areas with a conventional star topology is expected to become difficult from both cost and radio-congestion perspectives. A communication technique that addresses these issues is the mesh network. A mesh network interconnects multiple devices in a lattice-like topology and has recently been introduced into many IoT products. It is specified in numerous IoT-oriented wireless standards such as ZigBee [1], 6LoWPAN [2], Thread [3], and Matter [4]. Typical use cases span home automation scenarios, from temperature sensing and air-conditioner control to door lock, and adoption is advancing even in security-critical domains such as access control.

Moving Target Defense (MTD) [5] has attracted attention as a security technique for communication networks, including the Internet. MTD enhances security by dynamically altering system parameters such as identifiers exemplified by IP addresses or packet forwarding routes, making it harder for attackers to formulate a concrete attack strategy. This study focuses on the security of the IoT mesh network and proposes a robust security method for MTD-based mesh networks. The proposed approach seeks to minimize security impacts even when a malicious node joins the network while remaining simple enough to run on resource-constrained embedded devices. In addition, we implemented the method using Bluetooth as a prototype to emulate real-world wireless communication and evaluate its performance to verify its practical viability.

### C. Structure of this paper

The paper is structured as follows: Section II provides a background on the implementation of Route-Hopping MTD. We conclude with how MTD is usable for mesh networks. Section III introduces some related works and explains difference between the related works and this paper. Section IV then provides the Threat Model discussed in this paper. We then continue in Section V on the implementation of Route-Hopping MTD and then see the result of the metrics. Section VI provides a conclusion and gives an outlook.

## II. Background

### A. MTD

Moving Target defense (MTD) is a security technique that interferes with attackers by dynamically altering parameters—such as the identifiers of the resources being protected. The parameters subject to change can be broadly categorized as follows [5]:

- Identifiers used during communication (e.g., IP addresses, port numbers, MAC addresses).
- Communication paths used during packet forwarding.
- Software-execution environments (e.g., instruction sets, system-call numbers, Software Development Kits (SDKs).
- The software binaries themselves.

The primary objective of MTD is to heighten system complexity and parameter uncertainty, thereby increasing the difficulty of every stage from reconnaissance to exploitation and ultimately lowering an attacker's probability of success. By continually shifting system parameters, MTD raises the cost of reconnaissance and execution for adversaries while simultaneously reducing the likelihood that their attacks will succeed, thus strengthening overall system security.

### B. Mesh Network

A mesh network is a form of network topology in which every node is interconnected in a lattice-like (mesh) structure, and it is especially prevalent in IoT deployments. This architecture is widely employed for embedded systems, e.g., ZigBee [1] and 6LoWPAN [2]. Because nodes dynamically connect to one another in a mesh, communication with distant nodes can be achieved relatively inexpensively and with minimal complexity. In a mesh network, communication occurs when a packet travels from a source node to its destination by being forwarded through several intermediate (relaying) nodes. By virtue of its dynamically routed, interwoven links, a mesh network can deliver long-range connectivity, high reliability, and excellent scalability at low cost. The routing mechanism itself is described in a later section.

### C. Routing in Mesh Network

Ad hoc On-demand Distance Vector (AODV) protocol is a routing protocol widely employed for mesh networks [6]. AODV discovers packet paths by exchanging two control packets: Route Request (RREQ) and Route Reply (RREP). RREQ packets are forwarded via broadcast communication. The information included in an RREQ packet is as follows:

- Source address.
- Destination address.
- Sequence number.
- Cumulative communication cost.

RREP packets are forwarded via unicast communication. The information included in an RREP packet is as follows:

- Source address.
- Destination address.

In AODV, packet forwarding paths are discovered using the following procedure:

- The source node broadcasts an RREQ containing the destination's address to all immediate neighbors.
- Upon receiving the RREQ, each neighbor records a reverse route to the source using the header information and increments the cost metric to reflect the additional hop.
- The neighbor rebroadcasts the updated RREQ to its own neighbors.
- When an intermediate node receives an RREQ with the same sequence number it has already processed, it discards the duplicate; otherwise, it repeats the reverse-route recording and cost increment before forwarding.
- Steps 2–4 continue until the RREQ reaches the destination node.
- The destination may receive multiple RREQs; it retains only the one with the lowest cumulative cost and discards the others.
- The destination unicasts an RREP back toward the source along the reverse path stored in each intermediate node.
- When the source node receives the RREP, it caches the forward route, completing path setup so that data communication can begin.

In this way, each node—despite lacking a complete view of the entire path from source to destination—can still maintain the routing information needed to utilize the lowest-cost route. Each node can determine the next hop toward the destination node when forwarding a packet, thereby achieving shortest-path routing. Furthermore, RREP packets are delivered unicast along the routing information constructed in this procedure, and their reception signals that route discovery has completed. These mechanisms enable communication between non-adjacent nodes in a mesh network.

### D. Security concerns in mesh network

Several security challenges have been identified for mesh networks such as ZigBee. Olawumi et al. [7] report concrete security concerns in ZigBee and even demonstrate proof-of-concept attacks that exploit these vulnerabilities. The same study also highlights the risk of shared-key leakage from vulnerable devices. Because embedded systems typically face strict resource constraints, they often cannot adopt heavy-weight cryptographic mechanisms or Software-Defined Network (SDN)–based MTD techniques commonly used in general IT systems; as a result, securely storing shared keys may not always be feasible.

### *E. Value of implementing MTD in IoT domains*

Navas et al. [8] observe that IoT devices whose parameters tend to remain static over long periods are prone to security vulnerabilities. While the authors identify Moving Target Defense as an effective countermeasure, they also note that research on applying MTD specifically to IoT systems has not yet reached full maturity.

### *F. Multipath AODV and Route Hopping MTD for mesh networks*

Ikeda et al. [9] propose a Route-Hopping MTD scheme. Their approach enhances security by extending AODV to handle both route discovery and route selection. Specifically, multiple paths are discovered via broadcast during the discovery phase, and a route is chosen at random for each packet during forwarding, thereby improving security. Table 1 shows the results of the simulation implemented in Python. The authors implemented a simulation for the proposed method and tested its performance using the simulation. The results show that, in random number-based AODV, the route discovery time incurs only a slight overhead of about 6% respectively, compared to conventional AODV. Also, there is no overhead between simple AODV and packet id based AODV in route discovery. For packet forwarding, the performance of packet ID-based AODV remains nearly identical to that of ordinary AODV, whereas random number-based AODV introduces an additional overhead of approximately 7%. Although the evaluation was conducted only in software simulation, the results suggest that the overhead can be expected to remain sufficiently small. In this paper, we implement the proposed method and conduct a performance evaluation.

TABLE I. THE RESULTS OF SIMULATION

| (unit: ms) | AODV | packet id | random number |
|---|---|---|---|
| Discovery | 264 | 261 | 282 |
| Forwarding | 251 | 250 | 270 |

## III. RELATED WORK

### *A. Moving Target Defence in IP Networks*

Among the application domains of MTD, IP-network MTD is particularly well studied. The parameters chosen for alteration can vary, but they are generally grouped into two categories:

- Identifiers such as IP addresses and port numbers.
- Transmission-path settings such as routing tables [10].

To date, little work has explored dynamically modifying routing tables in mesh networks. A key reason is that embedded computers often cannot provide a sufficiently large and stable node population to support reliable route hopping. By contrast, the recent explosive growth of smart-home devices means that IoT mesh networks now contain enough nodes to make such path-switching increasingly practical.

### *B. SNR-Based multipath AODV method*

Park et al. [11] propose a multipath AODV scheme that selects the optimal route according to prevailing radio conditions. Like the present work, it discovers multiple paths via AODV, but then chooses the single route with the highest communication quality. An attacker, however, could manipulate that quality—e.g., by selective jamming—to steer traffic onto a path of their choosing, after which only that "best-quality" route would keep being used. Hence, the scheme is not considered conducive to improving security.

### *C. Moving Target Defence for Communication Technologies in IoT Devices*

Mercado-Velázquez et al. [12] propose an MTD technique that uses random communication methods in IoT devices. The proposed method distributes each device's traffic among Wi-Fi, BLE, ZigBee, and LoRa, and experiments confirm that security can be improved while limiting additional overhead such as CPU processing time to within 30 percent. However, the approach targets IoT devices that communicate directly with a server, so its applicability to the mesh networks examined in this paper is limited. Moreover, because each device must be equipped with multiple radio technologies, the method is unlikely to be practical for real-world products in terms of cost and power consumption.

### *D. Moving Target Defence for Communication Messages in IoT Devices*

Kusumi et al. [13] propose applying MTD to communications that use the Message Queuing Telemetry Transport (MQTT) protocol. MQTT follows a publish/subscribe model in which a single publisher node that generates data and multiple subscriber nodes that receive it communicate through a processing server called a broker. Designed as a lightweight protocol running over Transmission Control Protocol / Internet Protocol (TCP/IP), MQTT is well suited to relatively long-distance IoT communications that pass through an intermediary server.

Kusumi et al. introduce an MTD technique for MQTT in which the topics—identifiers that link publishers and subscribers to specific data streams—are periodically changed. By shuffling these tokens, the method makes it difficult for a malicious attacker to track a particular topic or device. The scheme also incorporates authentication and encryption, demonstrating that MTD can effectively reinforce security in MQTT-based systems.

The key difference between that prior work and the present study lies in their respective scopes and layers of defense.

The earlier research targets IoT communications that traverse a server and proposes an application-layer security mechanism, whereas our work focuses on direct device-to-device communication within a mesh network and enhances security by modifying network-layer routing mechanisms.

### *E. SDN Based route mutation for MTD*

Zhang et al. [14] introduce an MTD technique for wireless sensor networks which randomizes traffic between paths based on Software-defined networks. The proposed technique enhances security by forwarding requests and responses over disjoint paths, thereby increasing resilience against eavesdropping attacks. However, because it relies on Software-Defined Networking (SDN) controllers for dynamic path reconfiguration, the scheme is unsuitable for highly resource-constrained IoT devices.

### *F. OpenFlow Switch based MTD for sensor networks*

Anajemba et al. [15] also introduce an MTD technique for sensor networks which is based on OpenFlow Switches and changes packet paths periodically. This method enhances security by pre-configuring multiple communication paths on the OpenFlow switches and periodically switching to a different path for each communication interval. This approach is designed for IP networks and relies on Software-Defined Networking (SDN), which places an excessive load on IoT devices. Therefore, it cannot be applied to mesh networks built from low-cost devices.

## IV. Threat Model Assumed in this Paper

This section defines the assumed system environment, adversary model, and security objectives, thereby clarifying what requirements the proposed *Route-Hopping MTD* must satisfy and which threats it is designed to counter.

### *A. System Model*

The target system is a wireless mesh network composed of $n$ IoT devices, where $n$ ranges from ten to several hundreds. The underlying physical and link technologies are left unspecified. Also, we assume that any data exceeding a certain size is segmented into multiple packets before transmission.

### *B. Attacker Model*

The adversary can fully compromise up to $t$ *nodes* $(t \ll n)$ inside the network. A compromised node possesses the following capabilities, while all other nodes behave correctly:

- Evaesdropping, Modifying and Dropping packets.
- Modifying RREQ/RREP packets to attract packet routes to the malicious node itself.

The adversary is *not* assumed to perform, nor is the system required to defend against, the following:

- Large-scale Radio Frequency (RF) jamming that disrupts the entire network.
- Exploitation of software vulnerabilities such as buffer overflows—attacks that fall outside the scope of this study.

### *C. Security Goals*

The assets to be protected and the corresponding security goals are:

- Confidentiality and Integrity — Application payloads must remain undisclosed.
- Availability — The communication service should continue, keeping the Packet Delivery Ratio (PDR) as high as possible, even in the presence of compromised nodes.

and the following are not in the scope of this paper:

- Interception of packets at relay nodes and their decryption due to inadequate encryption.
- Software vulnerabilities like overflow not related to packet forwarding.

## V. Design of Route-Hopping MTD in Mesh Networks

### *A. Overview*

Previous work has paid only limited attention to MTD techniques for IoT devices, and the existing studies mainly focus on client-server communication security, not peer-to-peer style mesh network security. However, as IoT systems continue to expand, a robust security mechanism that can be applied to the mesh-network architecture will become essential, and MTD can be one promising candidate. Accordingly, this paper implements a lightweight Route-Hopping MTD scheme suitable for mesh networks suggested in [9]. We first explain the route-discovery procedure of the proposed method, and then describe two alternative strategies for selecting a path during packet forwarding.

### *B. Design Principles*

Route-Hopping MTD is designed as the extension to the ordinal AODV, covering two main aspects: route discovery and packet forwarding. First, during route discovery, our extended AODV discovers and stores multiple candidate routes whereas ordinal AODV retains only the single shortest path. Second, when packets are transmitted, the scheme dynamically switches among these stored routes on a per-packet basis, thereby realizing route hopping. Packet forwarding methods are as follows:

- Simple packet id based shuffling.
- Packet id based random number shuffling.

The detailed method will be described later.

### *C. Route Discovery*

Route discovery employs an enhanced version of AODV known as Multipath AODV. By extending the original protocol, this method can discover multiple routes instead of only the single lowest-cost path. Each node stores the N lowest-cost routes, according to the predetermined value of N. In our method, packet forwarding paths are discovered using the following procedure:

- The source node broadcasts an RREQ containing the destination's address to all immediate neighbors.

- Upon receiving the RREQ, each neighbor records a multiple reverse route to the source using the header information and increments the cost metric to reflect the additional hop.
- The neighbor rebroadcasts the updated RREQ to its own neighbors.
- When an intermediate node receives an RREQ with the same sequence number it has already processed, it stores up to N next-hop entries in ascending order of cost. It also updates the cost metric to record the additional hop.
- Steps 2–4 continue until the RREQ reaches the destination node.
- The destination may receive multiple RREQs; the destination node keeps the N lowest-cost next-hop entries.
- The destination broadcasts an RREP back toward the source along the reverse paths with the same manner as RREQ.
- When the source node receives the RREPs, it caches the forward routes, completing paths setup so that data communication with multiple routes can begin.

### D. Route Selection and Packet Forwarding

After multiple routes have been discovered, each node has to choose one node among them when forwarding a packet. In this proposed method, the nodes determine the route based on the specific packet id. We tried two concrete approaches for selecting the packet forwarding route:

- Simple packet id-based: Given a packet identifier *pid* and the total number of stored routes $N$, the next hop is selected by computing

  $$\text{index} = (pid \bmod N) + 1$$

  and the packet is forwarded along the *index*-th route in the routing table. This method is very lightweight and is very usable for resource-limited embedded systems, but the next route is easy to be guessed so the security level is lower than the random number based method described below.
- Packet id- and random number- based: Given a packet identifier pid, the total number of stored routes N, and Random Number Calculation Function

  $$\text{Random}(seed)$$

  the next hop is selected by computing

  $$\text{index} = (\text{Random}(pid) \bmod N) + 1$$

  and the packet is forwarded along the *index*-th route in the routing table. This method needs some calculations and might be heavier compared to the simple packet id method, but it can achieve higher security level because the next route is getting hard to guess. The impact of performing additional processing is evaluated in Section IV, Subsection C based on the simulation results.

### E. Summary and Open Issues

Research on Moving Target Defense (MTD) on networks has been widely explored in the context of IP networks, focusing on altering identifiers such as IP addresses and ports or dynamically adjusting routing tables. However, these approaches generally assume resource-rich environments and are not directly applicable to IoT mesh networks. In the IoT domain, several studies have examined the application of MTD, for example by switching between multiple wireless technologies or modifying application-layer tokens in protocols such as MQTT. While these approaches demonstrate security benefits, they often rely on devices equipped with multiple radio interfaces or the presence of centralized servers, which limits their applicability in low-cost, resource-constrained mesh topologies.

Other research has extended AODV to multipath discovery, often using criteria such as signal strength to select the best route. Although effective in improving communication quality, these methods remain vulnerable to adversaries capable of manipulating perceived channel conditions, and therefore do not fully address the security problem. Similarly, SDN-based MTD techniques provide flexible route mutation, but their reliance on centralized controllers makes them unsuitable for lightweight IoT deployments.

With respect to Route-Hopping MTD specifically, previous studies have investigated its potential through simulation, showing that dynamically alternating paths can reduce the probability of an attacker consistently intercepting packets. However, to the best of our knowledge, no prior work has implemented and evaluated Route-Hopping MTD in real communication systems or on actual IoT devices. This gap highlights the lack of empirical evidence on its practicality and effectiveness in real-world mesh networks.

In summary, the existing body of work highlights two key gaps. First, most prior research remains either at the simulation stage or targets scenarios with more capable devices, leaving open the question of how MTD can be realized in practice on resource-limited IoT mesh networks. Second, while multipath discovery has been studied, only limited attention has been paid to leveraging route hopping strategies as a direct security mechanism at the network layer in mesh environments. Addressing these gaps motivates the present study.

## VI. Implementation and Evaluation of the Proposed Method

### A. Implementation Overview

To evaluate the routing algorithm described above, we implemented the prototype with Bluetooth and Raspberry Pi and evaluated its performance. In this section, we explain the implementation and performance evaluation results.

### B. Architecture

The hardware and software used in our evaluation are as follows:

- Raspberry Pi 4 * 5 units.

- OS: Raspbian 12 Bookwarm.
- Software: Python 3.13 with Pybluez library.
- Radio: Bluetooth LE.

The software architecture is shown in Figure 1. To balance prototype development with algorithmic research, the developed software is a two-layer structure which consists of a routing algorithm layer and a Hardware Abstraction Layer (HAL). The routing algorithm layer is the core software and performs route discovery and next hop determination, while the HAL is replaceable software which is responsible for communication over real protocol stacks such as BLE and TCP.

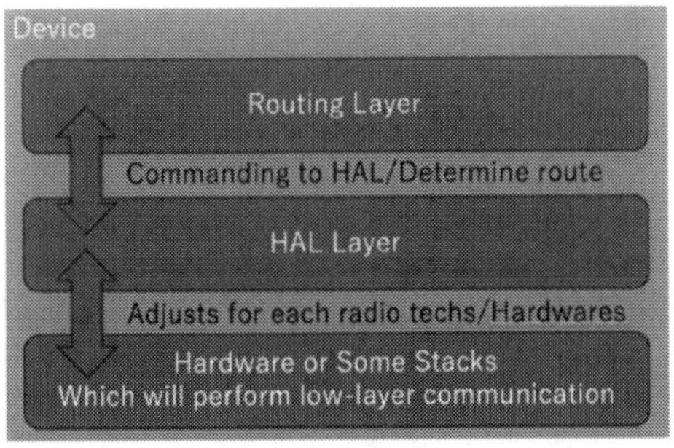


Figure 1. Route Hopping MTD Architecture.

### C. Performance Evaluation

We evaluated the performance of the network and measured some metrics. Measurements were performed ten times, and the average value was calculated. The network structure is shown in Figure 2. We measured the total time of route discovery and one-packet forwarding. The results are shown in Table 2. Route discovery is done with minimal overhead compared to the simple AODV method. Packet forwarding is done with very little overhead compared to the simple AODV method.

Figure 2. Network architecture for lightweight evaluation.

TABLE II. THE RESULTS OF EVALUATION

| (unit: ms) | AODV | packet id | random number |
|---|---|---|---|
| Discovery | 318 | 382 | 379 |
| Forwarding | 129 | 130 | 130 |

### D. Security Evaluation

In terms of security, the system now exhibits sufficiently high resilience against threats of the kind specified in the threat model. The threat model assumed the presence of malicious nodes. Assuming there are X independent paths and malicious nodes are present on T of them, the probability that a packet traverses a malicious nodes is

$$P = T/X$$

and if the sender sends the same packet twice, the possibility that two packets both traverse malicious nodes is

$$P = T/X * (T-1)/(X-1).$$

Also, if a large amount of data is being transmitted in several packets, the possibility that all packets traverse malicious nodes is

$$P = \prod_{i=0}^{P_{num}-1} \frac{T-i}{X-i}.$$

From these equations, it is evident that the likelihood of an attacker successfully intercepting or disrupting all packets decreases rapidly as the number of available disjoint paths $X$ increases. In other words, even if malicious nodes are distributed in the network, the probability of complete compromise becomes negligibly small once multiple independent routes are available. This stands in contrast to conventional AODV routing, where a single fixed path is repeatedly used and thus vulnerable to persistent attacks on that route. Moreover, the probabilistic distribution of packets across multiple routes creates uncertainty for adversaries. This uncertainty forces an attacker to compromise a significantly larger portion of the network in order to achieve the same level of disruption as in a static routing scheme. Consequently, the proposed scheme demonstrates clear security improvements by minimizing the success probability of attacks under realistic adversarial conditions.

### E. Discussion

Based on the performance evaluation, Route-Hopping MTD is expected to be achievable without incurring significant performance overhead. The evaluation confirmed that the additional processing time incurred during packet forwarding by this method remains minimal, suggesting that the approach is applicable even in scenarios demanding higher real-time performance. Moreover, the security evaluation indicates that the approach is especially effective in enhancing security for large-scale mesh networks.

## VII. CONCLUSION AND OUTLOOK

### A. Conclusion

In this paper, we implemented Route-Hopping MTD and carried out a performance evaluation. The results show that the overhead remained sufficiently small. Security testing confirmed a substantial improvement in resilience. Together, these findings indicate that Route-Hopping MTD is a practical and effective security measure for IoT devices.

### B. Future Works

These results demonstrate the usefulness of Route-Hopping MTD. However, we have yet to evaluate its performance in large-scale networks, and questions remain as to whether communication can be completed within practical time frames and whether memory and CPU consumption stay sufficiently low. Also, as future work, we plan to build a higher-fidelity simulation environment based on the metrics obtained in the present study and conduct more comprehensive experiments. Also, we will need to carry out a formal analytical evaluation of how memory and CPU consumption scale.

## ACKNOWLEDGEMENT

This study was supported by JST K Program Grant Number JPMJKP24K3, Japan and Hitachi Systems.

## REFERENCES

[1] "Ieee standard for local and metropolitan area networks–part 15.4: Low-rate wireless personal area networks (lr-wpans)," *IEEE Std 802.15.4-2011 (Revision of IEEE Std 802.15.4-2006)*, pp. 1–314, 2011. DOI:10.1109/IEEESTD.2011.6012487.

[2] "Ieee standard for low-rate wireless networks corrigendum 1: Correction of errors preventing backward compatibility," *IEEE Std 802.15.4-2020/Cor 1-2022 (Corrigendum to IEEE Std 802.15.4-2020 as amended by IEEE Std 802.15.4z-2020, IEEE Std 802.15.4w-2020, IEEE Std 802.15.4y-2021, and IEEE Std 802.15.4aa-2022)*, pp. 1–22, 2023. DOI:10.1109/IEEESTD.2022.10014667.

[3] *Thread specification, revision 1.3.0*, Available: https://www.threadgroup.org/ThreadSpec, Thread Group, Inc., 2023.

[4] *Matter 1.2 specification*, Available: https://csa-iot.org/all-solutions/matter/, Connectivity Standards Alliance (CSA), 2023.

[5] Y. W. X. Zhou Y. Lu and X. Yan, "Overview on moving target network defense," *2018 IEEE 3rd International Conference on Image, Vision and Computing (ICIVC)*, pp. 821–827, 2018.

[6] Z. Sun, X.-G. Zhang, D. Ruan, H. Li, and X. Pang, "A routing protocol based on flooding and aodv in the zigbee network," in *2009 International Workshop on Intelligent Systems and Applications*, 2009, pp. 1–4. DOI:10.1109/IWISA.2009.5072672.

[7] O. Olawumi, K. Haataja, M. Asikainen, N. Vidgren, and P. Toivanen, "Three practical attacks against zigbee security: Attack scenario definitions, practical experiments, countermeasures, and lessons learned," in *2014 14th International Conference on Hybrid Intelligent Systems*, 2014, pp. 199–206. DOI:10.1109/HIS.2014.7086198.

[8] R. E. Navas, F. Cuppens, N. Boulahia Cuppens, L. Toutain, and G. Z. Papadopoulos, "Mtd, where art thou? a systematic review of moving target defense techniques for iot," *IEEE Internet of Things Journal*, vol. 8, no. 10, pp. 7818–7832, 2021. DOI:10.1109/JIOT.2020.3040358.

[9] Y. Ikeda and H. Koide, *Implementing route-hopping mtd for iot mesh networks*, Japanese, Mar. 2025. [Online]. Available: https://ipsj.ixsq.nii.ac.jp/api/records/2001195.

[10] J. Narantuya *et al.*, "Sdn-based ip shuffling moving target defense with multiple sdn controllers," in *2019 49th Annual IEEE/IFIP International Conference on Dependable Systems and Networks – Supplemental Volume (DSN-S)*, 2019, pp. 15–16. DOI:10.1109/DSN-S.2019.00013.

[11] J. Park, S. Moh, and I. Chung, "A multipath aodv routing protocol in mobile ad hoc networks with sinr-based route selection," in *2008 IEEE International Symposium on Wireless Communication Systems*, 2008, pp. 682–686. DOI:10.1109/ISWCS.2008.4726143.

[12] A. A. Mercado-Velázquez, P. J. Escamilla-Ambrosio, and F. Ortiz-Rodríguez, "A moving target defense strategy for internet of things cybersecurity," *IEEE Access*, vol. 9, pp. 118 406–118 418, 2021. DOI:10.1109/ACCESS.2021.3107403.

[13] K. Kusumi and H. Koide, "Mqtt-mtd: Integrating moving target defense into mqtt protocol as an alternative to tls," in *2024 7th International Conference on Advanced Communication Technologies and Networking (CommNet)*, 2024, pp. 1–8. DOI:10.1109/CommNet63022.2024.10793300.

[14] B. Zhang and L. Han, "Dynamic random route mutation mechanism for moving target defense in sdn," Jun. 2021, pp. 536–541. DOI:10.1109/ISCIPT53667.2021.00114.

[15] J. Anajemba *et al.*, "Dsphr: A dynamic sdn-based port hopping routing technique for mitigating sd-wsn attacks," Apr. 2024. DOI:10.1007/s11277-024-10979-7.

# Integrating Cybersecurity and Digital Marketing Effectiveness: Exploring Resilience in Small to Medium-Sized Enterprises in Scotland

Kathy-Ann Fletcher
Faculty of Design, Informatics and Business
Abertay University
Scotland, United Kingdom
e-mail: k.fletcher@abertay.ac.uk

Nicole Carle
Faculty of Design, Informatics and Business
Abertay University
Scotland, United Kingdom
e-mail: n.carle@abertay.ac.uk

***Abstract*— As Small to Medium-sized Enterprises (SMEs) adopt digital marketing strategies to drive market growth, they face heightened exposure to cybersecurity threats. Through a qualitative methodology involving semi-structured interviews with SMEs in Scotland, the study identifies key themes including digital maturity, cybersecurity awareness, user trust, industry-specific challenges, and implementation barriers. Findings reveal a significant gap between cybersecurity awareness and practical implementation. The study proposes a model to guide SMEs in embedding cybersecurity into their marketing, thereby enhancing their resilience.**

***Keywords- SMEs; cybersecurity; digital marketing; data protection; readiness.***

## I. Introduction

This paper presents an exploration of the relationship between cybersecurity readiness and digital marketing effectiveness among Small and Medium-sized Enterprises (SMEs). These two variables are increasingly essential to the resilience of SMEs with [1] defining organisational resilience as "an organisation's capability for turning adverse conditions into an organisational opportunity, positive attitude of 'bouncing back' and a relatively agile deportment". This investigation covers challenges, identifies common vulnerabilities, and evaluates cybersecurity adoption from the perspective of the Technology Acceptance Model (TAM) illustrating the factors that build perceptions of ease of use and usefulness of cybersecurity protocols for SME digital marketing objectives. Studies have demonstrated the power of digital marketing tools (e.g., social media) by SMEs to improve brand visibility, customer acquisition, and operational efficiencies [2]. However, this increasing reliance on digital platforms exposes SMEs to a more sophisticated range of cybersecurity threats. There is the need for SMEs to have readiness strategies that align marketing innovation with cybersecurity resilience, which is the focus of this study. These strategies are important to build resilience into the SMEs themselves and the wider society as it protects against financial, reputational, social, and broader harms as identified by [3] and [4]. This paper will explore the literature review in Section II, the methodology in Section III, findings and analysis in Sections IV and V, discussion in Section VI, and conclusion and future work in Section VII.

## II. Literature Review

### *A. The Adoption of Digital Marketing by SMEs*

Extant research acknowledges the power of digital marketing as an enabler of customer acquisition but also of long-term relationship management [5] by fostering innovation and agility in business models, particularly in resource-constrained environments [6]. Fear of the security of digital marketing tools can limit the adoption of e-commerce and digital marketing [7]. According to the research, the fear of data breaches, phishing attacks and the intimidation posed by data protection regulations like General Data Protection Regulation - GDPR (2018) and Data Protection Act (2018) [8]. Loo et al. [7] note that some SMEs will perceive digital platforms as a risk due to their limited capacity to mitigate against cybersecurity threats. This limits their ability to benefit from the full range of digital marketing tools such as marketing automation, customer relationship management systems, and online advertising platforms. This aligns with Technology Acceptance Model (TAM) [9] by showing their attitude towards adopting cybersecurity protocols. The Perceived Usefulness (PU) and Perceived Ease of Use (PEOU) reflect a user's attitude towards using a system which then influences their behavioural intention to use and then their ultimate use of technology [10].

### *B. Cybersecurity Challenges for SMEs*

Larger enterprises often have dedicated Information Technology (IT) security teams or the ability to outsource expertise, formal risk management protocols, and the resources to invest in advanced cybersecurity infrastructure, which may not be available to SMEs [11]. This leaves SMEs targets for bad actors who commit phishing, malware, data breaches, account takeovers, and other cyber-attacks [12], [13]. While SMEs face a heightened risk due to their limited cybersecurity adoption and over-reliance on third-party digital platforms [12], Jahankhani et al. [15] emphasise the role that digital tools have in wider market reach which complicates the security risks for SMEs. These challenges are amplified by SME underestimation of cyber risk [14] and a lack of compliance with industry and regulatory standards such as GDPR or ISO/IEC 27001 [12], [15]. Research needs to consider the systemic harm caused by the human factor, which represents a critical weakness [16], [17], [18] to organisational resilience. This danger exists at various levels from management lack of cybersecurity readiness and strategy to employee lack of literacy [14] and buy-in, posing a risk to the resilience of organisations by exploiting the trust and routine business process to cause harms to the SMEs and their stakeholders [17], [19].

SMEs frequently lack formal cybersecurity policies or governance structures [20]. The absence of internal frameworks and policies as well as industry-wide or governmental policies and infrastructure is critical to the level of unpreparedness identified in SMES [21], [22]. The challenges include insider threat being one of the more dangerous [23], [24]. This threat comes from employees, contractors or partners who have access to internal systems and data [25]. These threats can be malicious or unintentional [26], highlighting the crucial need for training, awareness, and monitoring of threats from the SME [25]. SMEs are particularly vulnerable to insider threat [27], [28], due to their high trust and low oversight operations which gives employees broad access to sensitive systems and little role-based access controls [29].

### *C. Integrated Cybersecurity Readiness and Digital Marketing Effectiveness Model for SME resilience*

SMEs, which are adopting digital tools for their operational success [30], now need to embed cybersecurity into their marketing strategies. Cybersecurity strategies that work to secure customer data, ensure platform integrity and train marketing teams on cyber hygiene practices [12], hold immense potential to build trust between the company and its stakeholders. Consumer trust is a strategic asset [31], [32] where data privacy and integrity are paramount [33]. Research identifies several instruments by which cybersecurity builds trust. Firstly, [29] posits that trust is nurtured by transparency and systematic communication of security policies and data handling practices and breach response protocols. Secondly, authentication and access control protocols are signals to customers that their data is safeguarded [34], as they are strong identity and access management systems. Consequently, privacy protection and encryption are important for consumer trust especially in industries that manage sensitive data [35], [36]. Further, [37] notes the importance of detecting and mitigating threats early, which demonstrates a proactive approach to cybersecurity and reassures customers in the ability of the organisation in protecting their interests. Research like that discussed in [38]'s systematic review showed that compliance with international standards and participation in cybersecurity information sharing networks build trust by demonstrating accountability and collaboration. Considering all these identified links between cybersecurity, trust, and digital marketing [39], [40], it is imperative that cybersecurity is treated as a strategic business tool.

### *D. Research Gaps*

There are robust cybersecurity frameworks such as ISO/IEC 27001, GDPR and advice provided by the National Institute of Standards and Technology (NIST), however, SMEs face significant barriers to implementation [19]. For instance, SMEs are prioritising business growth and customer acquisition over investing in cybersecurity, which is seen as a cost [41], [42], [43]. In so doing, they miss the relationship between cybersecurity and their business goals of growth, profitability, and customer acquisition. The research in [44] argues that SMEs are failing to match their digital marketing ambitions to the technical and regulatory demands of the noted cybersecurity frameworks. Frameworks might mandate responsible practices like ethical data handling [45] and small firms either may be unaware of their responsibilities or lack the cybersecurity tools to operationalise them effectively [15]. This, therefore, creates a gap between intent and actual practice of cybersecure digital marketing, which undermines consumer trust, exposes businesses to reputational and legal risks, threatening their resilience and long-term viability. To address this gap, there are calls for simplified, SME-specific adaptations of frameworks based on usability, affordability, and ethical alignment. This study explores the relationship between cybersecurity and effective digital marketing practices in the context of SME resilience in Scotland.

### *E. Technology Acceptance Model (TAM)*

TAM has been widely applied across diverse disciplinary domains, [46], [47], [48], [49]. TAM was originated by [9], building on the Theory of Reasoned Action [50] and was designed to explain user acceptance of email technologies. Within TAM, the perceptions of users: Perceived Usefulness (PU) - the belief that a technology enhances performance [9], [51] - and Perceived Ease of Use (PEOU) - the belief that the technology requires minimal effort, shape their attitudes, which in turn influence behavioural intention and actual system use [52]. Although TAM is often praised for its simplicity [53], it has evolved to address its limitations. TAM2 [54] introduced social influence and cognitive instrumental processes, while the Unified Theory of Acceptance and Use of Technology [55] integrated multiple models to include performance expectancy, effort expectancy, social influence, and facilitating conditions. TAM3 [56] further incorporated perceived enjoyment and self-efficacy. Despite its widespread use, TAM has faced criticism. Scholars such as [57] and [58] argue that it overlooks contextual, cultural, and longitudinal factors. Others highlight its overreliance on self-reported data [59] and its individualistic orientation [60]. Additionally, [61] notes the model's neglect of variables like trust, perceived risk, and social norms. Nonetheless, TAM remains a foundational framework in technology adoption research. This study builds on TAM by adapting it to explore the relationship between cybersecurity readiness and digital marketing effectiveness - addressing a key gap by incorporating contextual variables.

## III. Methodology

To address the research gaps, identified in the literature review, this paper discusses the qualitative research undertaken for the project. We completed ten semi-structured interviews with key decision-makers from SMEs in various industries, including marketing executives, IT representatives, and owners. The sample was recruited through chambers of commerce members, SME organisations, and social media. The interviews were analysed using thematic analysis, developed by [62].

## IV. Findings and Analysis

The qualitative research interviews identified themes around digital marketing practices, cybersecurity awareness and industry-specific challenges faced by SMEs.

### *A. Theme 1: Digital Marketing Practices*

The organisations vary in their adoption of digital marketing, from basic social media use to advanced search engine optmisation and analytics. This displays varying levels of digital maturity around SMEs, with some further progressing in digital adoption than others. However, their success is measured based on the purpose of SMEs in using digital marketing. These measures include engagement, awareness, increased sales, and subscription in addition to financial return on investment. The respondents identify a shared growing intent to align public relations, communications, and digital strategies. With this shared intention, the need for rigorous industry-specific cybersecurity protocols for SMEs is growing.

### *B. Theme 2: Cybersecurity Awareness and Practices*

The participants demonstrate awareness of cybersecurity protocols that range from basic understanding to more structured practices. They more consistently use external IT support with some internal training. However, formal cybersecurity policies at an institutional level were lacking amongst the respondents. Many are only now beginning to take cybersecurity seriously as they perceived themselves as low-risk targets. They also mostly did not consider themselves targets, even in the face of digital marketing use, not previously making the link between the two variables.

### *C. Theme 3: User Trust and perception*

The respondents display a strong link between trust in digital platforms and customer engagement. Trust is a signal to the audience that websites are secure, and the branding is consistent, which is crucial for user engagement. The SMEs owners are aware of this link as their users are increasingly cautious about data sharing and cookies, especially on unfamiliar platforms. Trust is important beyond engagement but also allows users to share financial details and donate money to causes supported by the SME. This trust can be essential even in the aftermath of an attack to allow users to perceive that the company took all the precautionary steps to prevent the attack and will take accountability in the case of a successful threat.

### *D. Theme 4: Industry-Specific Challenges*

The respondents demonstrate several industry-specific challenges to adopting both digital marketing and cybersecurity protocols. Firstly, most of the organisations interviewed operate with limited financial and human resources that can be dedicated to improving either their digital outreach or cybersecurity. Participant B agreed that their SME is a soft target, but they do not have a large budget for cybersecurity. This implies that relying on external IT support creates gaps in responsibility, accountability, and awareness, creating the industry-specific gap in awareness and implementation. Despite these limited resources, some of the SMEs are handling extremely sensitive data, such as personal information of vulnerable individuals.

### *E. Theme 5: Barriers and Gaps*

The responses show a lack of formal training and industry-wide communication regarding formal cyber security protocols. Even with external IT support, this does not extend to internal training, capacity-building, or awareness. The human factor creates a weak link in the SMEs cybersecurity. This is related to a lack of clear roles about who is responsible for what within the cybersecurity, meaning SMEs are under the impression that it is being handled at some point, resulting in gaps in implementation. Even with awareness of resources, such as National Cyber Security Centre (NCSC) guidance or Charity Excellence Framework, these often go underutilised by the respondents, reflecting a gap between available support and the practical application of recommendations within these resources. Another barrier is that some SMEs did not see cybersecurity as a pressing concern, especially if they do not see themselves as targets or if they have not had any cybersecurity incidents. The lack of industry-wide dialogue or collaboration on cybersecurity is also a barrier. Without shared standards or peer learning threatening SMEs on an individual and industry-wide basis do not have the ability to plan and recover from cyberattacks, therefore, posing a real risk to their organisational resilience.

## V. Summary of Key Findings

SMEs measure digital marketing success through purpose-built metrics such as engagement and sales. There is a growing intention to integrate PR, communications, and digital strategies with robust cybersecurity protocols. SMEs show increasing awareness of cybersecurity but often lack formal policies and underestimate their vulnerability, which contributes to complacency and inconsistency in implementation of cybersecurity protocols. SMEs recognise that secure, consistent branding and transparency are vital to managing user confidence and loyalty. Unique challenges such as limited financial and human resources restrict SMEs' adoption of cybersecurity measures as they make use of the digital platforms to manage their customer relationships. The lack of formal training, internal capacity and industry-wide collaboration are further unique barriers to effective cybersecurity in SMEs.

## VI. DISCUSSION

Theme 1 revealed varying levels of digital maturity among SMEs. This aligns with TAM's construct of Perceived Usefulness (PU), where technology is adopted based on its potential to enhance performance [9], [51]. Theme 2 highlighted a gap between cybersecurity awareness and implementation. This implementation gap is critical, as cybersecurity readiness influences digital marketing effectiveness and overall resilience. This readiness and implementation gap is linked to the resource challenges identified by authors like [12] and [15]. The assumption that external IT support covers all cybersecurity needs reflects a lack of internal ownership, which undermines the organisation's ability to respond to disruptions. Venkatesh and Davis [54] expanded TAM to include social influence and job relevance, suggesting that organisational context shapes technology adoption—a factor often ignored in relation to SMEs. Theme 3 underscored the importance of user trust in digital platforms, linking it to engagement and other positive outcomes including resilience, diverging from arguments made by [61] that TAM neglects variables such as trust and perceived risk. Regarding resilience, trust is a strategic asset that empowers SMEs to recover from cyber-attacks while maintaining stakeholder confidence.

Theme 4 revealed that SMEs are faced with unique challenges due to their limited resources and the high data sensitivity of the services they provide. Despite handling vulnerable user data, many organisations lacked industry-specific cybersecurity frameworks. Authors of works like [57] and [58] critique TAM for failing to address contextual and cultural factors, a gap that this study addresses by adapting TAM to the specific case of resource-constrained industries. This study suggests that organisational resilience in these contexts would be improved with tailored guidance and shared standards. Theme 5's findings revealed barriers such as informal training, accountability gaps, and poor utilisation of available resources for improving cybersecurity implementation. This finding supports arguments that there are gaps in TAM's model, where it fails to predict sustained use and organisational integration [59] [60]. The lack of industry wide dialogue further isolates SMEs, affecting their resilience. This places the insight from industry wide dialogue as a crucial resource for SMEs that is useful for building capacity and safeguarding digital marketing operations.

## VII. CONCLUSION AND FUTURE WORK

This study has explored the critical intersection between cybersecurity readiness and digital marketing effectiveness within SMEs, highlighting the importance of integrating these domains to enhance organisational resilience. Through qualitative interviews and thematic analysis, the research identified key challenges including limited resources, low internal cybersecurity capacity, and a disconnect between awareness and implementation. The findings underscore the strategic value of cybersecurity not only as a protective measure but also as a trust-building tool that supports digital engagement and long-term viability.

By adapting the Technology Acceptance Model (TAM), the study offers an evaluation of the context of SME adoption of cybersecurity protocols within their digital marketing strategies. This adaptation addresses gaps in traditional TAM applications by incorporating variables such as trust, perceived risk, and organisational context—factors that are particularly relevant to SMEs operating in resource-constrained environments.

Future research should focus on developing simplified cybersecurity frameworks tailored to SMEs, aligning security practices with marketing goals and ethical data handling. Quantitative validation of the adapted TAM model across sectors would enhance its applicability, while longitudinal studies could assess the long-term impact of integrated cybersecurity-marketing strategies on resilience. Additionally, exploring industry-wide collaboration and policy support could foster a culture of cybersecurity, and targeted training initiatives may help address internal capacity gaps and reduce human-factor vulnerabilities. By bridging the gap between cybersecurity and digital marketing, this research contributes to a more holistic understanding of SME resilience and offers a foundation for future innovation, policy development, and academic inquiry.

## ACKNOWLEDGMENT

This work was supported by funding from the Carnegie Trust for the Universities of Scotland.

## REFERENCES

[1] D. Kantur and A. İşeri-Say, "Organizational Resilience: A Conceptual Integrative Framework," Journal of Management & Organization, 18(6), pp. 762–773, 2012, Available at: 10.1017/S1833367200000420.

[2] J. R. Saura, D. Palacios-Marqués and D. Ribeiro-Soriano, "Digital Marketing in SMEs Via Data-Driven Strategies: Reviewing the Current State of Research," Journal of Small Business Management, 61(3), pp. 1278–1313, 2023, Available at: 10.1080/00472778.2021.1955127.

[3] I. Agrafiotis, J. R. C Nurse, M. Goldsmith, S. Creese and D. Upton, "A Taxonomy of Cyber-Harms: Defining the Impacts of Cyber-Attacks and Understanding How they Propagate," Journal of Cybersecurity, 4(1), pp. 1, 2018, Available at: 10.1093/cybsec/tyy006.

[4] E. Islam, C. Rudolph and G. Oliver, "Managing Cyber Harm: A Survey of Challenges, Practices, and Opportunities,"

Information Security Journal, pp. 1–31, 2025, Available at: 10.1080/19393555.2025.2484348.

[5] S. Habib, N. N. Hamadneh and A. Hassan, "The Relationship between Digital Marketing, Customer Engagement, and Purchase Intention via OTT Platforms," Journal of Mathematics (Hidawi), 2022 (1) Available at: 10.1155/2022/5327626.

[6] N. Laila, P. Sucia Sukmaningrum, W. A. Saini Wan Ngah, L. Nur Rosyidi and I. Rahmawati, "An In-Depth Analysis of Digital Marketing Trends and Prospects in Small and Medium-sized Enterprises: Utilizing Bibliometric Mapping," Cogent Business & Management, 11(1), p. 2336565, 2024.

[7] M. K. Loo, S. Ramachandran and R. N. Raja Yusof, "Systematic Review of Factors and Barriers Influencing E-Commerce Adoption among SMEs over the Last Decade: A TOE Framework Perspective," Journal of the Knowledge Economy, 2024, Available at: 10.1007/s13132-024-02257-5.

[8] K. K. Kapoor, K. Tamilmani, N. P Rana, P. Patil, Y. K. Dwivedi and S. Nerur, "Advances in Social Media Research: Past, Present and Future," Information Systems Frontiers, 20, pp. 531-558, 2018.

[9] F. D. Davis, "Perceived Usefulness, Perceived Ease of Use, and User Acceptance of Information Technology," MIS Quarterly, pp. 319-340, 2018.

[10] F. Abdullah, R. Ward and E. Ahmed, "Investigating the Influence of the Most Commonly Used External Variables of TAM on Students' Perceived Ease of Use (PEOU) and Perceived Usefulness (PU) of e-portfolios," Computers in Human Behaviour, 63, pp. 75–90, 2016, Available at: 10.1016/j.chb.2016.05.014.

[11] U. Awan, A. Keprate and P. Braathen, "A Conceptual Framework of An Integrative Leadership for Cybersecurity Management and Designing Digital Road Map for Organizations," Digital Transformation, Routledge India, pp. 47-59, 2025.

[12] A. Papathanasiou, G. Liontos, A. Katsouras, V. and E. Glavas, "Cybersecurity Guide for SMEs: Protecting Small and Medium-Sized Enterprises in the Digital Era" Journal of Information Security, 16(1), pp. 1–43, 2025, Available at: 10.4236/jis.2025.161001.

[13] F. D. De Arroyabe, J. C. Arroyabe, M. Fernandez and C. F. A. Arranz, "Cybersecurity Resilience in SMEs. A Machine Learning Approach," The Journal of Computer Information Systems, 64(6), pp. 711–727, 2024, Available at: 10.1080/08874417.2023.2248925.

[14] C. R. Junior, I. Becker, and S. Johnson, "Unaware, Unfunded and Uneducated: A Systematic Review of SME Cybersecurity," arXiv preprint, 2023, Available at: arXiv:2309.17186.

[15] H. Jahankhani, L. N. K. Meda and M. Samadi, "Cybersecurity Challenges in Small and Medium Enterprise (SMEs) 'Blockchain and Other Emerging Technologies for Digital Business Strategies," Switzerland: Springer International Publishing AG, pp. 1–19, 2022.

[16] U. D Ani, H. He and A. Tiwari, "Human Factor Security: Evaluating the Cybersecurity Capacity of the Industrial Workforce," Journal of Systems and Information Technology, 21(1), pp. 2–35, 2019 Available at: 10.1108/JSIT-02-2018-0028.

[17] N. C. Edeh, "Cybersecurity and Human Factors," Cybersecurity for Decision Makers. 1st edn. United Kingdom: CRC Press, pp. 45–56, 2023.

[18] J. R. C. Nurse, "Cybercrime and You: How Criminals Attack and the Human Factors That They Seek to Exploit," The Oxford Handbook of Cyberpsychology, Ithaca: Oxford University Press, 2018.

[19] M. Wilson, S. McDonald, D. Button and K. McGarry, "It Won't Happen to Me: Surveying SME Attitudes to Cyber-security," The Journal of Computer Information Systems, 63(2), pp. 397–409, 2023, Available at: 10.1080/08874417.2022.2067791.

[20] B. Saha and Z. Anwar, "A Review of Cybersecurity Challenges in Small Business: The Imperative for a Future Governance Framework," Journal of Information Security, 15(1), pp. 24–39, 2024, Available at: 10.4236/jis.2024.151003.

[21] A. Chidukwani, S. and P. Koutsakis, "Cybersecurity Preparedness of Small-to-Medium Businesses: A Western Australia Study with Broader Implications," Computers & Security, 145, pp. 104026, 2024, Available at: 10.1016/j.cose.2024.104026.

[22] M. Neri, F. Niccolini and L. Martino, "Organizational Cybersecurity Readiness in the ICT Industry: a Quanti-Qqualitative Assessment," Information and Computer Security, 32(1), pp. 38–52, 2024, Available at: 10.1108/ICS-05-2023-0084.

[23] A. S. Abdullah, S. Dhiman and A. Ansari, "A Robust Model for Enabling Insider Threat Detection and Prevention: Techniques, Tools and Applications," Securing the Digital Frontier, Hoboken, NJ, USA: John Wiley & Sons, Inc, pp. 133–168, 2025.

[24] N. Ayanbode, O. A. Abieba, N. Chukwurah, O. O. Ajayi and A. I. Daraojimba, "Human Factors in Fintech Cybersecurity: Addressing Insider Threats and Behavioural Risks," International Journal of Multidisciplinary Research and Growth Evaluation, 5(1), pp. 1350–1356, 2024, Available at: 10.54660/.IJMRGE.2024.5.1.1350-1356.

[25] U. Inayat, M. Farzan, S. Mahmood. M. F. Zia, S. Hussain and F. Pallonetto, "Insider threat mitigation: Systematic Literature Review," Ain Shams Engineering Journal, 15(12), pp. 103068, 2024.

[26] A. Jaiswal, P. Dwivedi and R. K. Dewang, "Machine Learning Approaches to Detect, Prevent and Mitigate Malicious Insider Threats: State-Of-The-Art Review," Multimedia Tools and Applications, 2024, Available at: 10.1007/s11042-024-20273-0.

[27] A. Moneva and R. Leukfeldt, "Insider Threats among Dutch SMEs: Nature and Extent of Incidents, and Cyber Security Measures," Journal of Criminology, 56(4), pp. 416–440, 2023, Available at: 10.1177/26338076231161842.

[28] S. Pawar and H. Palivela, "LCCI: A Framework for Least Cybersecurity Controls to be Implemented for Small and Medium Enterprises (SMEs)," International Journal of Information Management Data Insights, 2(1), pp. 100080, 2022.

[29] A. Pigola, and F. de Souza Meirelles, "Unraveling Trust Management in Cybersecurity: Insights from a Systematic Literature Review," Information Technology and Management, 2024, Available at: 10.1007/s10799-024-00438-x.

[30] M. R. I. Bhuiyan, M. R. Faraji, M. Rashid, M. K. Bhuyan, R. Hossain and P. Ghose, "Digital Transformation in SMEs Emerging Technological Tools and Technologies for Enhancing the SME's Strategies and Outcomes," Journal of Ecohumanism, 3(4), pp. 211-224, 2024.

[31] L. Oliveira and M. Johanson, "Trust and Firm Internationalization: Dark-side Effects on Internationalization speed and How to Alleviate them," Journal of Business Research, 133, pp. 1–12, 2021, Available at: 10.1016/j.jbusres.2021.04.042.

[32] D. Koehn, "Integrity as a Business Asset", Journal of Business Ethics, 58(1/3), pp. 125–136, 2005, Available at: 10.1007/s10551-005-1391-x.

[33] A. Das, "Developing Dynamic Digital Capabilities in Micro-Multinationals Through Platform Ecosystems: Assessing the Role of Trust in Algorithmic Smart Contracts," Journal of International Entrepreneurship, 21(2), pp. 157–179, 2023, Available at: 10.1007/s10843-023-00332-7.

[34] W. Said, E. Mostafa, M. Hassan, and A. Mohamed Mostafa, "Multi-Factor Authentication-Based Framework for Identity Management in Cloud Applications," Computers, Materials & Continua, 71(2), pp. 3193–3209, 2022, Available at: 10.32604/cmc.2022.023554.

[35] N. J. King and V.T. Raja, "Protecting the Privacy and Security of Sensitive Customer Data in the Cloud," Computer Law & Security Review, 28(3), pp. 308–319, 2012, Available at: 10.1016/j.clsr.2012.03.003.

[36] Z. Morić, V. Dakic, D. Djekic and D. Regvart, "Protection of Personal Data in the Context of E-Commerce," Journal of Cybersecurity and Privacy, 4(3), pp. 731–761, 2024, Available at: 10.3390/jcp4030034.

[37] M. Tahmasebi, "Beyond Defense: Proactive Approaches to Disaster Recovery and Threat Intelligence in Modern Enterprises," Journal of Information Security, 15(2), pp. 106–133, 2024, Available at: 10.4236/jis.2024.152008.

[38] R. Posso and J. Altmann, "Trust and Trust-Building Policies to Support Cybersecurity Information Sharing: A Systematic Literature Review," International Conference on the Economics of Grids, Clouds, Systems, and Services, Cham: Springer Nature Switzerland, pp. 212-228, 2024.

[39] H.N. Şenyapar, "Digital Marketing in the Age of Cyber Threats: A Comprehensive Guide to Cybersecurity Practices," Journal of Social Science, 8(15), pp. 1–10, 2024, Available at: 10.30520/tjsosci.1412062.

[40] L. Bhagyalakshmi, "Securing the Future of Digital Marketing through Advanced Cybersecurity Approaches and Consumer Data Protection Privacy and Regulatory Compliance," Journal of Cybersecurity & Information Management, 13(1), 2024.

[41] M. Tsiodra, S. Panda, M. Chronopoulos, and E. Panaousis, "Cyber Risk Assessment and Optimisation: A Small Business Case Study," IEEE Access, 11, pp. 1, 2023, Available at: 10.1109/ACCESS.2023.3272670.

[42] A. Chidukwani, S. Zander and P. Koutsakis, "A Survey on the Cyber Security of Small-to-Medium Businesses: Challenges, Research Focus and Recommendations," IEEe Access, 10, pp. 85701-85719, 2022.

[43] M. Dinkova, R. El-Dardiry and B. Overvest, "Should Firms Invest More in Cybersecurity?," Small Business Economics, 63(1), pp. 21–50, 2024, Available at: 10.1007/s11187-023-00803-0.

[44] M. F. Arroyabe, C. F. A. Arranz, I. F. De Arroyabe, and J. C. F. de Arroyabe, "Revealing the Realities of Cybercrime in Small and Medium Enterprises: Understanding Fear and Taxonomic Perspectives," Computers & Security, 141, pp. 103826, 2024, Available at: 10.1016/j.cose.2024.103826.

[45] K. Macnish and J. van der Ham, "Ethical Approaches to Cybersecurity," Oxford Handbook of Digital Ethics, Oxford University Press, 2023.

[46] D. A. Adams, R. R. Nelson and P. A. Todd, "Perceived Usefulness, Ease of Use, and Usage of Information Technology: A Replication", MIS Quarterly, pp. 227-247, 1992.

[47] A. L. Lederer, D. J. Maupin, M. P. Sena and Y. Zhuang, "TAM and the World Wide Web," AMCIS Proceedings, pp. 258, 1997.

[48] M. H. Alhumsi and R. A. Alshaye, "Applying Technology Acceptance Model to Gauge University Students' Perceptions of Using Blackboard in Learning Academic Writing," Knowledge Management & E-Learning, 13(3), pp. 316-333, 2021.

[49] Y. C. Huang, L.L. Chang, C.P. Yu and J. Chen, "Examining an Extended Technology Acceptance Model with Experience Construct on Hotel Consumers' Adoption of Mobile Applications," Journal of Hospitality Marketing & Management, 28(8), pp. 957-980, 2019.

[50] M. Fishbein and I. Ajzen, "The Theory of Reasoned Action as Applied to Moral Behaviour: A Confirmatory Analysis," Addison-Wesley Publishing Company, Reading, MA, 1975.

[51] S. Jeong, S. Kim and S. Lee, "Effects of Perceived Ease of Use and Perceived Usefulness of Technology Acceptance Model on Intention to Continue Using Generative AI: Focusing on the Mediating Effect of Satisfaction and Moderating Effect of Innovation Resistance," International Conference on Conceptual Modeling, Cham: Springer Nature Switzerland, pp. 99-106, 2024.

[52] F. D. Davis, R. P. Bagozzi, and P. R. Warshaw, "User Acceptance of Computer Technology," Journal of Management Science. 35 (8), pp. 982-1003, 1989.

[53] F. D. Davis and A. Granić, "Evolution of TAM," The Technology Acceptance Model. Human–Computer Interaction Series," Cham: Springer, 2024, Available at: https://doi.org/10.1007/978-3-030-45274-2_2.

[54] V. Venkatesh and F. D. Davis, "A Theoretical Extension of the Technology Acceptance Model: Four Longitudinal Field Studies," Management Science, 46(2), pp. 186-204, 2000.

[55] V. Venkatesh, M. G. Morris, G. B. Davis and F. D Davis, "User Acceptance of Information Technology: Toward a unified view," MIS Quarterly, pp. 425-478, 2003.

[56] V. Venkatesh, and H. Bala, "Technology acceptance model 3 and a research agenda on interventions," Decision sciences, 39(2), pp. 273-315, 2008.

[57] R. P. Bagozzi, "The Legacy of the Technology Acceptance Model and a Proposal for a Paradigm Shift," Journal of the Association for Information Systems, 8(4), p. 3, 2007.

[58] I. Benbasat, and H. Barki, "Quo vadis TAM?', Journal of the Association for Information Systems," 8(4), p.7, 2007.

[59] P. Legris, J. Ingham, and P. Collerette, "Why do People Use Information Technology? A Critical Review of The Technology Acceptance Model," Information & Management, 40(3), pp. 191-204, 2003.

[60] N. Marangunić and A. Granić, "Technology Acceptance Model: A Literature Review from 1986 to 2013," Universal Access in the Information Society, 14, pp. 81-95, 2015.

[61] A. Y. L. Chong, "Predicting M-Commerce Adoption Determinants: A Neural Network Approach," Expert Systems with Applications, 40(2), pp. 523-530, 2013.

[62] V. Braun and V. Clarke, "Using Thematic Analysis in Psychology", Qualitative Research in Psychology, 3(2), pp. 77–101, 2006.

# Temporary Identification Management System Using UNIX Time for IoT Device Privacy Protection

Koki Mizoguchi
Department of Informatics, The Graduate University for Advanced Studies
2–1–2, Hitotsubashi, Chiyoda-ku, Tokyo, 101–8430, JAPAN.
e-mail: mizoguchi-koki@nii.ac.jp

Somchart Fugkeaw
Sirindhorn International Institute of Technology, Thammasat University
131 M.5 Tiwanont Rd., Bangkadi, PathumThani, 12000, THAILAND.
e-mail: somchart@siit.tu.ac.th

Masahito Kumazaki, Hirokazu Hasegawa, Hiroki Takakura
Center for Strategic Cyber Resilience R&D, National Institute of Informatics
2–1–2, Hitotsubashi, Chiyoda-ku, Tokyo, 101–8430, JAPAN.
e-mail: {kumazaki,hasegawa,takakura}@nii.ac.jp

***Abstract*—With the rapid growth of Internet of Things (IoT) devices, privacy concerns regarding device identifiers have become increasingly significant. Authentication and Key Exchange (AKE) protocols are essential for securing IoT environments, but many implementations transmit device identifiers in plaintext or hashed form, which can lead to privacy issues for device users. On the other hand, session-based ID anonymization systems, which change device identifiers every time authentication occurs, require reading and writing on Non-Volatile Memory (NVM), such as flash memory, which consumes more energy and has limited write endurance. This paper proposes a novel ID management system for generating temporary device identifiers using UNIX time, which does not require reading and writing on NVM. The system is considered a communication and update process that is delay resilient. The effectiveness of the proposed system is also demonstrated in terms of computational and communication costs compared to three baseline systems. The proposed system is concluded to be one of the effective solutions for protecting the privacy of resource-constrained IoT devices and their users.**

***Keywords-IoT; Device Identifier; Privacy; ID anonymization; UNIX time.***

## I. INTRODUCTION

The global share of the Internet of Things (IoT) is increasing at an accelerating rate. Transforma Insights estimates that the number of IoT connections will reach 40.6 billion by 2034 [1]. Authentication and Key Exchange (AKE) protocols are essential to securing IoT environments. In most AKE protocols, IoT devices must provide their IDs to the authentication server for identification. IoT device IDs contain manufacturing information, such as the maker name, product model, and firmware version; hardware IDs, such as Media Access Control address (Mac address), International Mobile Equipment Identity (IMEI), and serial number; owner information, such as owner registered information and relationship with owner's account; and location information, such as installed location and local network IDs.

Until now, many AKE protocols have been proposed, and the ways of providing IDs of IoT devices are classified as plaintext, hashed, and session-based ID anonymization systems.

Messages repeatedly sent from the same devices result in the same hash value, even if the device identifier is hashed. It enables eavesdroppers to link different communications originating from the same devices. Eavesdroppers can recognize communication between specific IoT devices and authentication servers, observe the frequency and intervals of communication, and infer device usage patterns by observing the amount or size of transmitted data. Since many IoT devices exhibit regular and identifiable communication patterns based on user interaction, this information can be used to infer device usage patterns. For instance, a smart lock sends its hashed ID at a specific time every day, and eavesdroppers can infer the user's typical leave or return home time and the user's behavioral patterns. If it is easy to estimate original IDs, such as MAC address, phone number, and other regular and short IDs, a rainbow table attack and a dictionary attack are enabled. According to Choudhary [2], privacy concerns regarding device identifiers arise not only from the exposure of raw identifiers but also from the ability to associate seemingly anonymous data with behavioral patterns. It is emphasized that even anonymized or encrypted transmissions can leak sensitive information when analyzed over time.

Overall, plaintext and hashed IDs are not sufficient to protect the privacy of IoT devices and their users due to the risk of eavesdropping and inference of device usage patterns.

To address to prevent inference of device usage patterns using hashed IDs, session-based ID anonymization systems are proposed. In this systems, IDs are changed every time authentication occurs. The IoT device and the authentication server generate temporary IDs based on the state. This approach prevent inference of device usage patterns through eavesdropping on IDs, like plaintext and hashed IDs. However, it requires reading and writing operation on Non-Volatile Memory (NVM), such as flash memory, to store the state. Flash memory is representative of NVM, which is widely used in IoT devices. There are two concerns about using it. First, reading and writing on flash memory consumes more energy than volatile memory, such as DRAM [3][4]. Second, NVM exhibits limited write endurance, meaning it can only sustain a finite number of write operations before experiencing failure or degradation [5]. Ferroelectric RAM (FRAM/FeRAM) is a promising alternative to flash memory for non-volatile storage, offering higher endurance and lower energy consumption, though it remains more expensive and less widely available [4][6].

In summary, the plaintext and hashed IDs are not sufficient to protect the privacy of IoT devices and their users due to the risk of eavesdropping and inference of device usage patterns. Session-based ID management systems can protect the privacy of IoT devices and their users by changing IDs every time authentication occurs, but they require reading and writing on NVM, which consumes more energy and has limited write endurance.

To address these issues, this research proposes a new system to generate temporary IDs using UNIX time, which does not require reading and writing on NVM, and IoT devices' IDs are changed every certain times. UNIX time is used despite using state, which is synchronized between IoT devices and the authentication server. The generated temporary IDs are changed at certain times.

The paper is organized as follows: Section II describes related work and classification of ID management system. Section III describes the proposed system. Section IV provides a comparative evaluation of the proposed system against three baseline approaches, focusing on computational cost, communication overhead, and the achieved privacy level. Section V discusses the limitations of the proposed system and these potential solutions. Section VI concludes the paper.

## II. Related Work

This section describes related work on ID anonymization systems for IoT devices.

Braeken proposed a PUF-based P2P (Peer-to-Peer) AKE protocol for IoT devices [7]. In this protocol, the IoT devices' IDs are not anonymized but are in plaintext.

Badhib et al. proposed a robust CSS (Client Server System) AKE protocol for IoT devices [8]. This protocol adopts a session-based ID anonymization system. The IoT device sends its ID, which is masked with the shared key and track sequence, to the authentication server. They are changed every time authentication occurs. However, the protocol requires reading and writing on NVM to store them in the IoT device.

For large-scale smart IoT applications, Chen et al. proposed a novel authentication scheme that models and supports the entire lifecycle of IoT device authentication, from manufacturing to daily use and resetting [9]. However, the IoT device ID (denoted as the smart device's unique identity) is transmitted in plaintext.

Alizadeh et al. proposed anonymous ticket-based authentication protocol for the IoT [10]. In this protocol, the IoT device ID is anonymized using arias ID. The combination of a hashed ID, secret, and nonce is a critical component of the proposed protocol's approach to sensor anonymity. Specifically, each alias ID is meticulously constructed from a hashed ID, the Sensor Node's (SN) secret value (denoted as $ID_{SN}$), and a nonce. This intricate composition significantly impedes the identification of an object's true identity, as malicious actors would be required to possess knowledge of the object's secret to ascertain its real ID. Employing a one-way hash function for each object's ID renders its decoding practically unfeasible. However, provided with the context in which fixed IDs are transmitted, it becomes possible to collect information, such as the communication time and interval of specific devices.

Nimmy et al. proposed a PUF-based CSS AKE protocol for IoT devices [11]. This protocol also adopts a session-based ID anonymization system. The IoT device sends its ID, which is masked with the state, to the authentication server. The state is stored in the IoT device's NVM and changed every time authentication occurs.

Tun and Mambo proposed a PUF-based secure AKE protocol for IoT devices [12]. In this protocol, the IoT devices' IDs are not anonymized but are in plaintext.

## III. Proposed System

This section provides a detailed description of the proposed system. The notation used in this paper is shown in Table I.

TABLE I. Notation and Description

| Notation | Description |
|---|---|
| $H(x)$ | Apply hash function $H$ to $x$ |
| $a \leftarrow b$ | Assign $b$ to $a$ |
| $a \parallel b$ | Bitwise concatenate $a$ and $b$ |
| $\lfloor x \rfloor$ | Round down $x$ to the nearest integer |
| UNIX TIME | Current UNIX time |

### A. System Overview

The proposed system assumes an environment where many IoT devices are connected to an authentication server. Figure 1 shows the structural overview of the process. It denotes the authentication server possesses two types of processes: generation of temporary ID and identification by temporary ID. Figure 2 shows an example of the authentication server's database.

The authentication server stores the original ID, three types of temporary IDs, and data, such as the authentication information, in its database. When an IoT device requests authentication, it sends its temporary ID to the authentication server. The temporary ID is generated based on the IoT device original ID and the current UNIX time as follows:

$$\mathtt{id}_T \leftarrow H\left(\mathtt{id} \parallel \left\lfloor \frac{\mathtt{UNIX\ TIME}}{x} \right\rfloor\right) \quad (1)$$

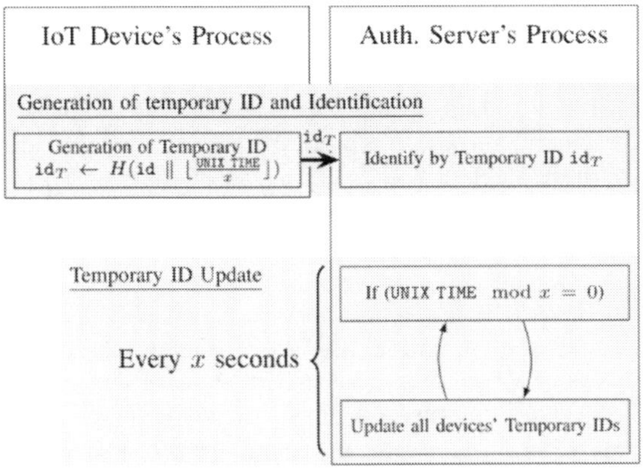


Figure 1. Structural overview of the process.

| id | $id_{T1}$ | $id_{T2}$ | $id_{T3}$ | data |
|---|---|---|---|---|
| 0x82... | 0x21... | 0x70... | 0x4F... | 0x93... |
| 0xEA... | 0x45... | 0x82... | 0x18... | 0xA7... |
| | | ⋮ | | |
| 0xD6... | 0x89... | 0xA3... | 0x28... | 0xC1... |

Figure 2. Authentication server database example.

where id is the IoT device original ID, $id_T$ is the temporary ID, and $x$ is the ID update interval constant shared between the IoT device and the authentication server. UNIX time is a system for tracking time, defined as the number of seconds that have elapsed since the Unix epoch, which is 00:00:00 UTC on 1 January 1970. The temporary ID $id_T$ is changed every $x$ seconds. This mechanism follows a principle similar to that of the Time-based One-Time Password (TOTP) algorithm [13]. Assuming the current UNIX time is synchronized between the IoT device and the authentication server. The condition on the value $x$ and consideration of the communication and update process delay are described in Section III-D.

### *B. Initialization Phase*

The IoT device original ID and ID update interval constant $x$ are shared in advance. The authentication server generates three types of temporary IDs in the initialization phase and saves its database:

$$\begin{aligned}
\mathtt{id}_{T1} &\leftarrow H\left(\mathtt{id} \parallel \left\lfloor \frac{\mathtt{UNIX\ TIME} - x}{x} \right\rfloor\right) && \text{Previous time-step,}\\
\mathtt{id}_{T2} &\leftarrow H\left(\mathtt{id} \parallel \left\lfloor \frac{\mathtt{UNIX\ TIME}}{x} \right\rfloor\right) && \text{Current time-step,}\\
\mathtt{id}_{T3} &\leftarrow H\left(\mathtt{id} \parallel \left\lfloor \frac{\mathtt{UNIX\ TIME} + x}{x} \right\rfloor\right) && \text{Next time-step.}
\end{aligned} \tag{2}$$

### *C. Temporary IDs Update Phase*

The authentication server updates the temporary IDs in its database every $x$ seconds. The temporary IDs are updated as follows:

$$\begin{aligned}
&\mathtt{id}_{T1} \leftarrow \mathtt{id}_{T2}, \qquad \mathtt{id}_{T2} \leftarrow \mathtt{id}_{T3},\\
&\mathtt{id}_{T3} \leftarrow H\left(\mathtt{id} \parallel \left\lfloor \frac{\mathtt{UNIX\ TIME} + x}{x} \right\rfloor\right).
\end{aligned} \tag{3}$$

To execute this operation every $x$ seconds, the condition

$$\mathtt{UNIX\ TIME} \mod x = 0 \tag{4}$$

is used. To enhance the performance of the authentication server, the previous time-step and current time-step temporary IDs are substituted with the current time-step and the next time-step temporary ID, respectively, instead of generating new temporary IDs as in Equation (2).

### *D. Communication and Update Process Delay*

Communication delay and the temporary ID update process delay on the authentication server should be considered.

The communication delay is the time it takes for the IoT device to send its temporary ID to the authentication server and for the authentication server to process it. The update delay is the time it takes for the authentication server to update its temporary IDs in its database.

In the following, the effectiveness of the proposed system in addressing these delays and the condition of ID update constant $x$ are discussed. The notation of the communication and update process delays is defined in Table II.

TABLE II. NOTATION OF COMMUNICATION AND UPDATE DELAY

| Notation | Description |
|---|---|
| $\Delta d$ | The communication delay. The IoT device sends $id_T$ to the authentication server, and it takes $\Delta d$ seconds to reach the authentication server. |
| $\Delta t$ | Time required to update all temporary IDs on the authentication server. |
| $\Delta t'$ | Time required to update a certain temporary ID on the authentication server. Assuming that the authentication server has 10,000 records on its database, the 5,000th record could be updated approximately $\Delta t' = \frac{1}{2}\Delta t$ seconds later. |

Three cases are considered based on the relationship between $\Delta d$, $\Delta t'$, and $\Delta t$. Figure 3 shows the three cases. In (a), the update delay is larger than the communication delay. In (b), the communication delay is larger than the update delay. In (c), the communication delay is larger than the update delay and update time of all temporary IDs. The gray area represents the time when the temporary ID is updated. This process assumes that, for a certain ID id, the authentication server takes $\Delta t'$ seconds to update the temporary ID $id_T$ in its database.

Consider the case where the time required to update a certain temporary ID exceeds the communication delay (see Figure 3 (a)). Regarding points P1, P2, and P4, $id_T$ sent from the IoT devices will match the current time-step temporary ID $id_{T2}$ in the authentication server's database. Regarding point P3, the IoT device sends $id_T$ using the current UNIX time, but the authentication server has not updated its temporary ID $id_{T2}$ yet. Thus, $id_T$ sent from the IoT device matches

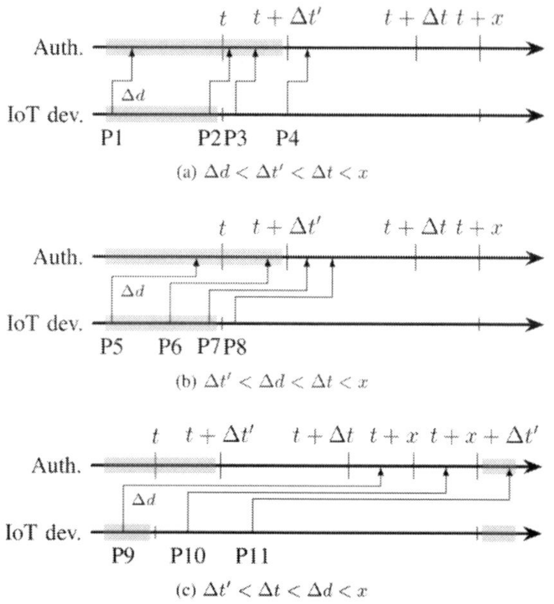


Figure 3. Update and communication delay.

the next time-step temporary ID $\mathtt{id}_{T1}$ in the authentication server's database.

Consider the case where the communication delay exceeds the time required to update a certain temporary ID. The time required to update all temporary IDs exceeds the communication delay (see Figure 3 (b)). Regarding points P5, P6, and P8, $\mathtt{id}_T$ sent from the IoT devices will match the current time-step temporary ID $\mathtt{id}_{T2}$ in the authentication server's database. Regarding point P7, the IoT device sends $\mathtt{id}_T$, but the authentication receives it after the update process is completed due to the communication delay. Thus, $\mathtt{id}_T$ sent from the IoT device matches the next time-step temporary ID $\mathtt{id}_{T3}$ in the authentication server's database.

Finally, consider the case where the communication delay exceeds the time required to update a certain temporary ID (see Figure 3 (c)). Regarding point P10, $\mathtt{id}_T$ sent from the IoT devices will match the current time-step temporary ID $\mathtt{id}_{T2}$ in the authentication server's database. Regarding points P9 and P11, the authentication server has not updated the IoT device temporary ID. Thus, $\mathtt{id}_T$ sent from the IoT device matches the previous next-step temporary ID $\mathtt{id}_{T3}$ in the authentication server's database.

Consequently, the authentication server can identify the IoT device by matching the temporary ID sent from the IoT device with the temporary ID in its database.

Concerning all cases, the ID update interval constant $x$ should be set to a value larger than the communication delay $\Delta d$ and the time required to update all temporary IDs $\Delta t$.

## IV. Evaluation

This section evaluates the computational and communication overhead of the proposed system and privacy level in comparison to three traditional ID management systems, incorporating authentication schemes commonly used in IoT systems. The comparison highlights the efficiency of the proposed method in terms of lightweight operations and minimal data exchange. Table IV summarizes the computational, communication costs and privacy level of the proposed system and three baseline as follows:

- **Baseline 1**: The IoT device sends its ID in plaintext.
- **Baseline 2**: The IoT device sends its ID in hashed form.
- **Baseline 3**: Assuming that the IoT device derives a masked ID using hash function from its original ID and stored mask value in its NVM. The mask value (32 bytes) is generated by the authentication server and sent to the IoT device every time authentication occurs in plaintext.

This process assumes that the hash function is a cryptographic hash function Secure Hash Algorithm 256-bit (SHA-256), which produces a 32 bytes output.

Table III defines the privacy levels regarding the ID management systems. The privacy level is defined based on the ability to track the IoT device over time and the reuse of the ID.

TABLE III. Privacy Level Definition

| Privacy Level | Description |
|---|---|
| None | The IoT device ID is sent in plaintext, allowing easy identification of the device. |
| Weak | The IoT device ID is not disclosed, but the ID is reused for multiple authentication sessions, making it possible to track the device over time. |
| Strong | The IoT device ID is changed every time authentication occurs or periodically, and the ID is not reused, making it difficult to track the device over time. The ID is masked with a secret value, enhancing privacy protection. |

TABLE IV. Comparison of Computational and Communication Costs, and Privacy Levels

| System | Computational Cost | | Communication Cost | Privacy Level |
|---|---|---|---|---|
| | IoT device | Auth. Server | | |
| Proposed | 1 hash, R UNIX TIME | $n$ hash every $x$ seconds, $\leq 3$ comparison | 1 message (32 bytes) | Strong |
| Baseline 1 | No cost | 1 comparison | 1 message (32 bytes) | None |
| Baseline 2 | 1 hash | 1 hash, 1 comparison | 1 message (32 bytes) | Weak |
| Baseline 3 | 1 hash, receive mask value, R/W NVM | 1 hash, generates mask value | 2 messages (64 bytes) | Strong |

**Abbreviations:**
$n$ is the number of IoT devices connected to the authentication server.
R/W is read and write, respectively.

As shown in Table IV, the proposed system offers the lowest computation and communication costs by utilizing a single hash function and unidirectional message transmission on the IoT device side. This design is highly suitable for resource constrained IoT environments. Although Baseline 1 incurs no computational cost and Baseline 2 has a similar cost to the proposed system on the IoT device side, their privacy protections can be described as none and weak, respectively, due to the reuse of static identifiers. On the other hand, Baseline 3 provides enhanced privacy by masking the ID, which can be described as strong, but incurs additional costs due to the need for generating and transmitting mask values.

Consequently, the proposed system achieves a balance between privacy protection and resource efficiency, making it a compelling choice for IoT applications where both computational and communication resources are limited.

## V. Discussion

This section discusses the limitations of the proposed system and these potential solutions.

### A. RTC Clock Drift

The proposed system uses UNIX time to generate temporary IDs and assumes that the IoT device and the authentication server have synchronized UNIX time. Most computers adopt the Real-Time Clock (RTC) to keep track of time. However, the RTC is not always accurate [14], and the clock drift–the offset between the actual time and the time kept by the RTC drift–can affect the correctness of generation of temporary ID.

Two approaches can be considered to address the clock drift issue. First, the IoT device can periodically synchronize its RTC with the authentication server's time using a time synchronization protocol, such as NTP (Network Time Protocol). In NTP, the IoT device and the authentication server communicate to NTP servers to synchronize their clocks. This approach helps maintain the accuracy of the IoT device's and the authentication server's RTC clocks. However, there are some concerns regarding the overhead and security of NTP. In terms of overhead, NTP imposes the need for IoT devices to perform write operations to the RTC registers in order to update the time values, in addition to incurring the communication overhead associated with the protocol. In terms of security, NTP does not ensure the authenticity of the time source, which may lead to the injection of falsified time information. According to Martin et al. [15], authentication in the context of NTP does not imply that the time is correct. Secure NTP [16] is a protocol that provides authentication and integrity protection for NTP messages, but it requires additional complexity and overhead for digital signatures and certificates.

Second, measure the offset between the IoT device's RTC and the authentication server's time denoted as $\Delta p$, and adjust the generation of temporary ID accordingly. The abstract of generation of temporary ID considering the clock drift is as follows:

1) Measure the round trip time (RTT) between the IoT device and the authentication server and obtain the average RTT denoted as $\overline{R}$.
2) The IoT device sends its RTC clock to the authentication server.
3) The authentication server calculates the offset between its RTC clock as follows:

$$\Delta p \leftarrow \text{IoT device's RTC} - \text{Auth. Server's RTC} - \frac{\overline{R}}{2}. \tag{5}$$

If $\Delta p > 0$, the IoT device's RTC is ahead of the authentication server's RTC, and if $\Delta p < 0$, the IoT device's RTC is behind the authentication server's RTC.
4) The authentication server stores the $\Delta p$ value associated with the IoT device's ID.
5) The authentication server generates and updates the temporary ID as follows:

$$\begin{aligned} &\mathtt{id}_{T1} \leftarrow \mathtt{id}_{T2}, \quad \mathtt{id}_{T2} \leftarrow \mathtt{id}_{T3}, \\ &\mathtt{id}_{T3} \leftarrow H\left(\mathtt{id} \parallel \left\lfloor \frac{\mathtt{UNIX\ TIME} + x + \Delta p}{x} \right\rfloor\right). \end{aligned} \tag{6}$$

This algorithm is executed every certain time interval. This approach only stores the offset of the time drift, eliminating the need for time synchronization via external servers such as NTP server. However, since the integrity of the RTC values transmitted by the IoT device cannot be guaranteed, it is necessary to incorporate mechanisms to ensure the integrity of the time information. The authentication server also requires the additional storage of the offset value $\Delta p$ for each IoT device.

Both approaches incur additional communication and processing overhead, resulting in increased energy consumption of IoT devices. This overhead depends on the frequency of RTC synchronization. Therefore, it is necessary to examine whether this overhead can be reduced in comparison with the Baseline 3 presented in Section IV, which relies on read and write operations to NVM.

### B. RTC Energy Consumption

There is a concern that the energy consumption of the RTC. The RTC consumes energy to keep track of the time. According to Nisshinbo Micro Devices Inc.[17], the RTC (C2051S01) is active for 10 years with a 3V CR2032 coin cell battery. RTC is designed to consume low power, and its energy consumption is negligible compared to the IoT device's energy consumption. However, it is necessary to measure the RTC's energy consumption and compare it with that of reading and writing to NVM, such as flash memory, in order to store temporary IDs.

### C. Scalability of the Authentication Server

The authentication server should be able to process the generation of temporary ID and identification by temporary ID. In the proposed system, the authentication server generates one next time-step temporary ID and two substitution operations every $x$ seconds for each device connected to the authentication server. Assuming that 100,000 IoT devices are connected to the authentication server, the authentication server needs to generate 100,000 next time-step temporary IDs and perform 200,000 substitution operations every $x$ seconds. It is predicted that this protocol requires the authentication server to have sufficient processing capacity to handle these operations efficiently.

## VI. Conclusion and Future Work

To address privacy concerns in IoT environments, this paper proposes an ID management system that leverages UNIX time to generate temporary device identifiers. In conventional systems, device IDs are often transmitted either in plaintext or in hashed form. This allows adversaries to monitor communication patterns and infer usage behavior over time, thereby introducing significant privacy risks. Moreover, session-based ID management schemes typically require frequent updates to NVM, resulting in increased energy consumption and reduced memory lifespan due to repetitive write operations.

In the proposed system, a temporary device ID is dynamically generated by computing a hash of the original device ID concatenated with the current UNIX timestamp. This temporary ID is updated every $x$ seconds, where $x$ is a shared constant known to both the IoT device and the authentication server. Since the identifier changes periodically, even successive communications from the same device appear to originate from different sources. This makes long-term tracking by eavesdroppers significantly more difficult. Furthermore, because ID updates are computed in memory without requiring writes to NVM, the scheme mitigates the energy and endurance issues inherent to session-based ID management systems. In the analysis conducted, the proposed system demonstrates lower computational and communication costs compared to traditional ID management systems, making it particularly suitable for resource-constrained IoT devices.

By integrating the system into the AKE protocol, the smart lock can be identified without revealing its original or static ID. Eavesdroppers cannot track the smart lock over time based on the temporary ID.

Future work will focus on two directions. First, the system will be implemented and evaluated on resource-constrained IoT devices (e.g., MCU, Micro Controller Unit) and authentication servers, measuring computational cost, energy consumption, and scalability under large device populations. These results will also inform the development of methods for determining the optimal update interval $x$, which is essential for balancing security and performance. Second, RTC clock drift will be investigated, comparing mitigation techniques to quantify their impact on the integrity and efficiency of the proposed approach.

Overall, these efforts will refine the system design and confirm its practicality for real-world IoT deployments, particularly in scenarios where energy efficiency and privacy-preserving authentication are critical.

## Acknowledgments

This research would not have been possible without the valuable guidance and continuous support of Professor Akihiro Shimizu of Kochi University of Technology, Japan. The authors are deeply grateful for his insightful advice throughout the course of this work. This work was partially supported by JST K Program Grant Number JPMJKP24K3, Japan.

## References

[1] Transforma Insights, "Current IoT Forecast Highlights," Accessed: Jun. 25, 2025. [Online]. Available: https://transformainsights.com/research/forecast/highlights.

[2] A. Choudhary, "Internet of Things: a comprehensive overview, architectures, applications, simulation tools, challenges and future directions," *Discover Internet of Things*, vol. 4, no. 1, p. 31, 2024.

[3] B. C. Lee, E. Ipek, O. Mutlu, and D. Burger, "Architecting phase change memory as a scalable dram alternative," in proceedings of *the 36th annual international symposium on Computer architecture*, 2009, pp. 2–13.

[4] M. Kim, J. Lee, Y. Kim, and Y. H. Song, "An analysis of energy consumption under various memory mappings for FRAM-based IoT devices," in proceedings of *2018 IEEE 4th World Forum on Internet of Things (WF-IoT)*, 2018, pp. 574–579.

[5] S. Bennett and J. Sullivan, "NAND flash memory and its place in IoT," in proceedings of *2021 32nd Irish Signals and Systems Conference (ISSC)*, 2021, pp. 1–6.

[6] J. Boukhobza, S. Rubini, R. Chen, and Z. Shao, "Emerging NVM: A survey on architectural integration and research challenges," *ACM Transactions on Design Automation of Electronic Systems (TODAES)*, vol. 23, no. 2, pp. 1–32, 2017.

[7] A. Braeken, "PUF based authentication protocol for IoT," *Symmetry*, vol. 10, no. 8, p. 352, 2018.

[8] A. Badhib, S. Alshehri, and A. Cherif, "A robust device-to-device continuous authentication protocol for the internet of things," *IEEE Access*, vol. 9, pp. 124 768–124 792, 2021.

[9] F. Chen, Z. Xiao, T. Xiang, J. Fan, and H.-L. Truong, "A full lifecycle authentication scheme for large-scale smart IoT applications," *IEEE Transactions on Dependable and Secure Computing*, vol. 20, no. 3, pp. 2221–2237, 2022.

[10] M. Alizadeh, M. H. Tadayon, and A. Jolfaei, "Secure ticket-based authentication method for IoT applications," *Digital Communications and Networks*, vol. 9, no. 3, pp. 710–716, 2023.

[11] K. Nimmy, S. Sankaran, and K. Achuthan, "A novel lightweight PUF based authentication protocol for IoT without explicit CRPs in verifier database," *Journal of Ambient Intelligence and Humanized Computing*, vol. 14, no. 5, pp. 6227–6242, 2023.

[12] N. W. Tun and M. Mambo, "Secure PUF-based authentication systems," *Sensors*, vol. 24, no. 16, p. 5295, 2024.

[13] D. M'Raihi, S. Machani, M. Pei, and J. Rydell, *Rfc 6238: Totp: Time-based one-time password algorithm*, 2011.

[14] R. Moravskyi and Y. Levus, "Using Stream Processing for Real-Time Clock Drift Correction in Distributed Data Processing Systems," in proceedings of *2024 IEEE 19th International Conference on Computer Science and Information Technologies (CSIT)*, 2024, pp. 1–4.

[15] J. Martin, J. Burbank, W. Kasch, and P. D. L. Mills, *Network Time Protocol Version 4: Protocol and Algorithms Specification*, RFC 5905, Jun. 2010. DOI: 10.17487/RFC5905.

[16] D. F. Franke, D. Sibold, K. Teichel, M. Dansarie, and R. Sundblad, *Network Time Security for the Network Time Protocol*, RFC 8915, Sep. 2020. DOI: 10.17487/RFC8915.

[17] Nisshinbo Micro Devices Inc., "Real Time Clock (RTC): Introduction," Accessed: Jun. 25, 2025. [Online]. Available: https://www.nisshinbo-microdevices.co.jp/en/products/real-time-clock/introduction/.

# A File Access Permission Management System to Realize Task Transfer during Cyber Attacks

Hidetoshi Kawai
Department of Informatics, The Graduate University for Advanced Studies, Tokyo, JAPAN
e-mail: h-kawai@nii.ac.jp

Masahito Kumazaki, Hirokazu Hasegawa, Hiroki Takakura
Center for Strategic Cyber Resilience R&D, National Institute of Informatics, Tokyo, JAPAN
e-mail: {kumazaki,hasegawa,takakura}@nii.ac.jp

Masahiko Kato
Department of Health Data Science, Juntendo University, Chiba, Japan
e-mail: m.kato.ug@juntendo.ac.jp

***Abstract*—When a cyberattack happens to any company, they often disconnect the attacked device or all of the devices in the department where the attack device belongs from the internal network. The primary objective of this study is to improve business continuity. In this paper, we propose a system for file access management under cyberattack. The system is designed to allow the transfer of file access permissions from a cyberattack victim to other employees. The system uses victim file information and staff information, and determines who to transfer authority to based on the file's content and importance, as well as the individual's expertise and reliability.**

***Keywords-Cyber Attacks; File access permissions; Reliability; Expertise; Business Continuity.***

## I. INTRODUCTION

When a cyber attack happens to any company, they often disconnect the attacked device from the internal network to respond to the incident. Sometimes, they have to disconnect multiple devices, and all operations using those devices will be suspended. However, in the case of the infrastructure, e.g., medical, transportation, electric power, communication, and so on, suspension of the attacked device may cause serious damage to our society. Therefore, the primary objective of this study is to improve business continuity under cyber attacks.

In the military, if a superior officer is injured and unable to continue their duties, their subordinates are promoted to take over to continue their work. Applying this to a company under cyberattack, the tasks previously handled by the compromised employee would be continued by their subordinate, who gets promoted. However, this method might not work if the subordinate does not have sufficient skills to perform those duties. Additionally, since these tasks are recorded in files, it is important to manage the file access permissions.

In this paper, we propose a file access permission management system under cyber attacks. The system aims to distribute the work of the employee who was attacked to others. First, it determines whether a subordinate can take over tasks based on the file content, considering factors like confidentiality. If it is decided that a subordinate can handle a file, that file is then assigned to an individual based on its importance, the employee's individual expertise, and their reliability, thus determining who will take over the superior's duties.

The outline of this paper is as follows. We introduce previous research related to file access permission management in Section II. Section III describes the proposed system, and Section IV explains the implementation plan, how to evaluate a pilot. In Section V, we discuss what needs to be improved in the pilot. Finally, we present our conclusion and future works in Section VI.

## II. RELATED WORK

It is important to protect sensitive information in every company and organization. A lot of methods to determine individual access privileges have been developed until today. Discretionary Access Control (DAC) has been used for a long time. DAC lets resource owners decide who can access their work. It is a flexible way to control who can access resources like files and databases because owners can give or take away permissions from other users [1]. Mandatory Access Control (MAC) is also used for accesses to highly confidential information in critical environments like military ones. MAC needed to have flexible access control mechanism with the development of computing technology [2]. However, DAC and MAC are not suitable for today's complex organizations [3]. So, the method called Role-based Access Control (RBAC) was proposed by Ferraiolo and Kuhn in 1992 [4] to solve the problem. This access control method centralizes management by role, and cannot be delegated between users without authority. Thus, it improved the file management efficiency compared to MAC and DAC. After that, RBAC has been studied using various approaches because researchers aimed to achieve one that reflected changing organizational circumstances. Julisch and Karjoth [5] presented an automated method for determining access permissions for new users or users whose roles have changed within an organization, focusing on the assignment of appropriate access rights. The proposed method assesses the access rights of similar users and decides new access permissions for new people in department positions. Moreover,

Privacy-aware Role-Based Access Control (P-RBAC) was proposed by Qunet al. as an evolution of RBAC [6]. It aimed to apply restrictions required by privacy laws and internal policies in an organization to RBAC.

Focusing on the fact that previous studies assumed that no cyber attacks had occurred, McGraw proposed a new access-control approach called Risk-Adaptable Access Control (RAdAC). RAdAC dynamically weighs mission importance against security risk and chooses the best information-sharing decision for each situation [7]. However, the system proposed by him has low adaptability to general organizations because it was developed for the military.

## III. Proposed System

### A. *Overview of the Proposed System*

We propose a file access permission management system to improve business continuity under cyber attacks. Figure 1 shows the concept of the proposed system in this paper.

When a victim device of a cyber attack is isolated from the network, the user of the device cannot push his work forward. It may not only be his problem but also cause a delay or business suspension in his department. Therefore, the system ensures business continuity in the department by dividing his work to other persons in his department. The proposal system determines a substitute person and changing access permissions from the victim to him for all files to which only the victim has access permission.

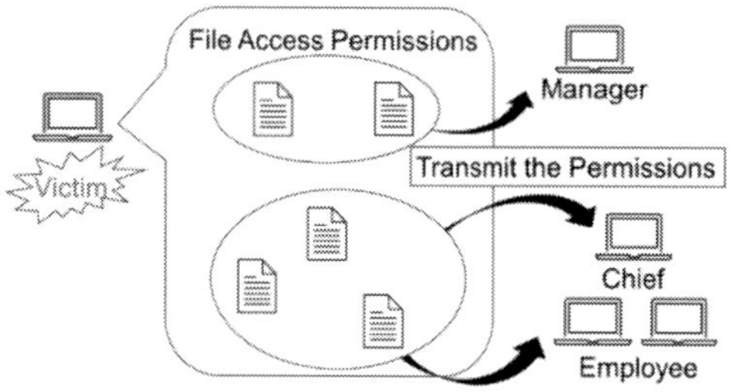


Figure 1. Concept of the Proposed System.

### B. *Assumption*

In order to determine the substitute worker of each file, the system uses information about files and staff. The detailed assumptions in this paper are listed below.

*1) Victim File Information:* The file information includes the list of victim's files with each file's data, importance, expertise it requires, and access permitted information. The victim's file is a file only the victim has write permission to. We describe the details of file's importance and expertise below.

- File Importance
  File Importance is based on three values, Confidentiality, Integrity, and Availability. It decides what positions have access to files according to the importance.
- File Expertise
  This expertise is the value that reflects the level of skill required to operate files. This value is decided by the owner who has the file access permissions.

*2) Staff Information:* The Staff Information consists of name, staff ID, department, post, IP address, reliability, and user expertise. IP address and staff ID are linked and managed on the Asset Management DB. Moreover, Staff Information without IP address is consolidated and stored in the Human Resources Information DB. In particular, we describe the reliability and expertise below.

- Reliability
  Reliability is a score that quantifies each user's level of security awareness and risk. Shinoda et al. proposed a method to calculate the reliability based on multiple indicators [8]. In this method, Carelessness, Awareness of Efforts to Secure, and Security Skill Levels are used for the calculation of reliability. The Carelessness is calculated based n the results from the Security Surprise Test, URL Filtering Detection, and Incident History. The Awareness is determined based on the Progress Rate of Security Training Courses and the response of the Security Surprise Test. The User Skill Level is decided based on the Test Result Scores during Security Training Courses and the result of the Security Surprise Test. We assumed that Reliability of each user has been calculated in advance using this method and is available as part of the Staff Information.
- User Expertise
  User Expertise refers to very high domain-specific competence relative to peers with the same tasks in a specific domain [9]. In other words, User Expertise represents how skilled a person is at their job compared to their colleagues. For example, an employee in the Development department needs programming skill, technical knowledge, and more. User Expertise indicates these values per employee in this example. It is assumed that User Expertise related to the duties of the department to which each user currently belongs is calculated and included in the staff information.

### C. *Architecture*

Figure 2 shows the architecture of the proposed system. The system consists of three modules, Information Collector, Access Permission Allocator, and OverWriter. These modules play a role in collecting information about users and files, deciding new file access permissions, and overwriting the new permissions. The Access Permission Allocator module consists of five components: Contents Classifier, Importance Classifier, Expertise Classifier, Reliability Classifier, and File Permission Decider. Figure 3 shows these components in the Access Permission Allocator.

*1) Information Collector:* First, the administrator who manages this proposed system inputs the IP address of the victim device in the Information Collector Module when an attack is detected (Figure 2 - I). By using the IP address of the victim's device, Asset Management provides this module with the staff ID of the device owner who was attacked (Figure 2 - II, II′). Subsequently, it obtains victim information about Reliability, Department, and Post with staff ID from Human Resources Information (Figure 2 - III, III′). Using the staff ID, it searches the file server for files only the victim has

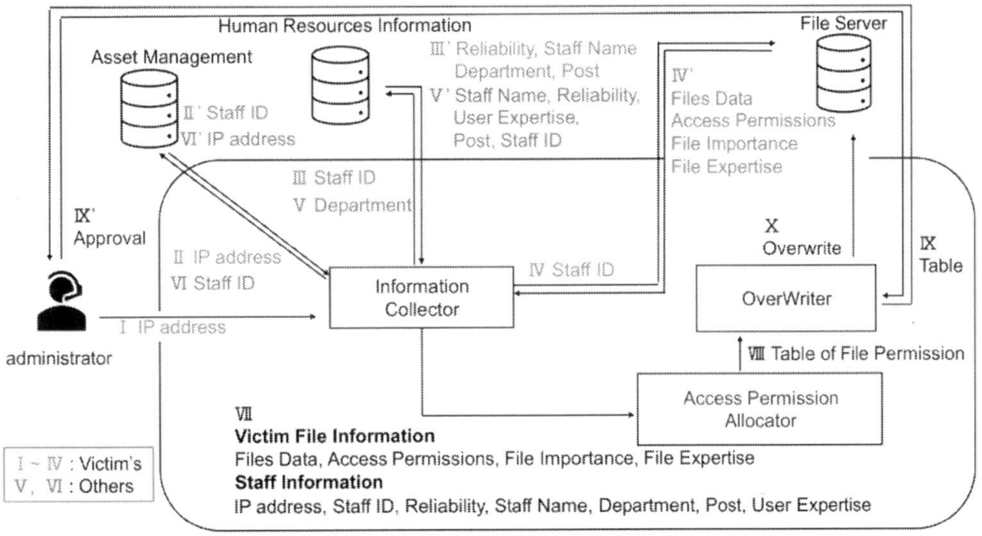


Figure 2. Architecture of the Proposed System.

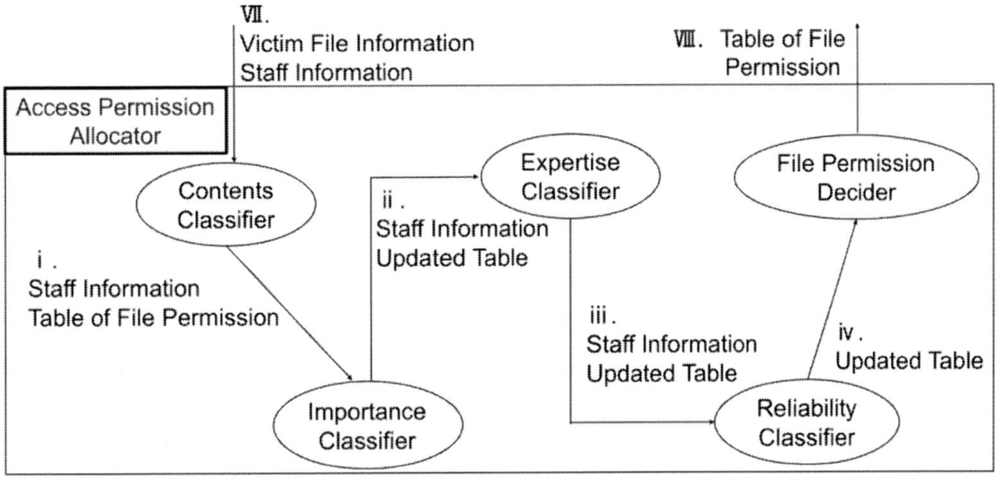


Figure 3. Components in Access Permission Allocator.

permission to write to and gathers the files found together with their importance and expertise information (Figure 2 - I V, IV′). Based on the gathered files, it generates Victim File Information.

In addition, the module collects Staff Information of all members in the same department as the victim by victim's department (Figure 2 - V, V′). It sends all the ID of collected Staff Information to Asset Management DB and receives the IP addresses if their device (Figure 2 - VI, VI′). Finally, the module sends Staff Information consisting of the victim and all members of his department with their device's IP address and Victim File Information to the Access Permission Allocator module (Figure 2 - VII).

*2) Access Permission Allocator:* The module consists of five components and Figure 3 shows the structure of the module. Each component performs classifying the victim's file permissions to decide new permissions according to the information received from previous module. The details are as follows.

- Contents Classifier

  This component classifies the file access rights according to the file contents and makes a table of new file permissions. Files that only victim can access include highly classified information. For instance, that needs approval of the position above the victim, is recorded in the minutes of the executive meeting, and more. Of course, there is also no classified information. For this reason, we have to check these files, whichever victim's subordinates can access or not, based on the contents of victim's file in Staff Information (Figure 3 - i ). In order to analyze the contents, this component utilizes Large Language Model (LLM) because it is so difficult to analyze them that are not standardized format and written in natural language. That is why this component uses LLM to analyze the contents and this module makes a table of individuals who may be granted file access permission, and sends it next to the components.

- Importance Classifier
  This component modifies the importance of files that are allowed to pass file permissions to subordinates by the previous component. When the victim cannot use his device and his subordinates have to operate his work, there are gaps in access permissions based on file importance. So, this component temporarily changes his file importance and determines the extent to which permissions are to be redistributed among his subordinates. In order to do it, the component decreases the importance of the file by one level and eliminates the gap. At last, the component updates the table received from the previous module and sends it to the next component (Figure 3 - ii).
- Expertise Classifier
  Expertise Classifier Component decides someone who is not enough to operate the victim's file based on the expertise his subordinates have. This process narrows down the candidates to whom file permissions may be distributed based on the user expertise, and file access permissions will be distributed only to staff who meet the required technical capabilities. In addition, the required technical level is determined for each file, and this value is compared with the staff's expertise to determine whether to grant access to the file. The component then changes the table to show this process and sends it to the next component (Figure 3 - iii).
- Reliability Classifier.
  This component decides his subordinates are not reliable according to the reliability score because this component aims to prevent them from distributing file permissions to low trust staff by narrowing them. It compares victim's Reliability Score with his subordinate's score and update the table from previous component (Figure 3 - iv).
- File Permission Decider
  The above components have been narrowed down the victim's subordinates to whom file access permissions are distributed. This component decides who will have access to the files in accordance with the amount of work for an individual. This decision is reflected in a table, and the component updates the table that links the IP addresses of the devices owned by each subordinate. Finally, this component sends it to the OverWriter module (Figure 3 - VIII).

*3) OverWriter:* OverWriter module receives the table from Access Permission Allocator module (Figure 2 - VIII), and sends it to the administrator who manages the system to get approval. After he approves it, the module replaces the victim's file permissions with the new one (Figure 2 - IX, IX′, X).

## IV. Evaluation

The proposed system is still in the idea stage and has not yet been implemented. Therefore, we conducted a simulation to verify the system. This paper discusses its expected results.

### *A. Evaluation Method*

Figure 4 shows the network of an assumed experimental organization. There are five devices and people in each of the two departments. We assume the section manager of department A is attacked, and our proposed system will distribute file access permissions from the section manager to others. In addition, victim file information is on the File Server, and his files are categorized into three levels of importance based on the policy of Information-technology Promotion Agency, Japan (IPA) [10]. The IPA has stipulated that the importance of a file is determined by assessing it on a three-level scale for each of the criteria of confidentiality, integrity, and availability, and then determining the importance based on the maximum value of each of these levels. He deals with six files, and these files consist of two of each file with a level one, level two, and level three importance. Moreover, the Asset Management DB is on the Asset Management Server, and the Human Resources Information DB is on the Human Resources Information Server, as shown in Figure 4. Especially, Table I is a part of staff information in the Human Resources Information DB and represents the personnel deployment in the organization.

TABLE I. Part of Staff Information

| Staff ID | Staff Name | Post | Department |
|---|---|---|---|
| A1 | | Manager | A |
| A2 | | Section Manager | A |
| A3 | | Chief | A |
| A4 | | Employee | A |
| A5 | | Employee | A |

### *B. Expected Results*

In this subsection, we explain about the expected results and the interim one. Access Permission Allocator module receives victim file information and staff information from Information Collector module, and outputs the table of file permission to OverWriter module. Table IV is the output from Access Permission Allocator module, and Table II and Table III are the interim table from any components in this module.

Table II is the interim table generated by Reliability Classifier components. Components from Contents Classifier to Reliability Classifier decide someone who cannot access the victim's files following file contents, file importance, user expertise, and reliability, and this table reflects these decisions. The details are shown below.

- File 1 :
  People without Manager whose staff ID is A1 cannot access the file based on file contents, file importance, user expertise, and reliability.
- File 2, 3, 4 :
  Only employees whose staff ID are A4 and A5 cannot access these files.
- File 5, 6 :

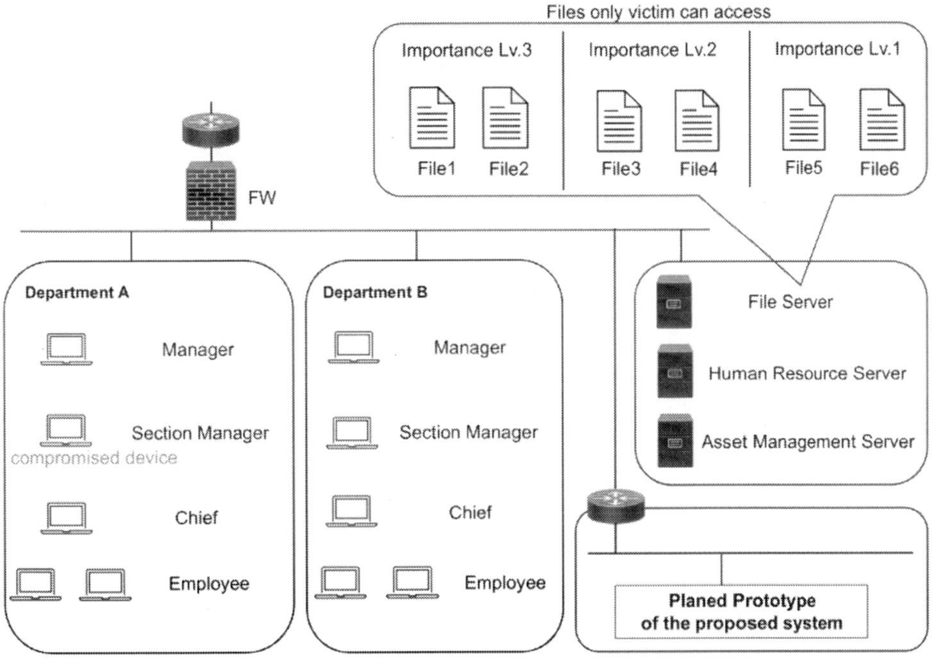


Figure 4. Assumed Experimental Network.

TABLE II. ACCESS OR NOT TABLE BY RELIABILITY CLASSIFIER

| | Staff in Department | | | |
|---|---|---|---|---|
| Files | A1 | A3 | A4 | A5 |
| File1 | - | x | x | x |
| File2 | - | - | x | x |
| File3 | - | - | x | x |
| File4 | - | - | x | x |
| File5 | - | - | - | - |
| File6 | - | - | - | - |

√ : access, x : no access,

- : undecided

TABLE III. ACCESS OR NOT TABLE BY FILE PERMISSION DECIDER

| | Staff in Department | | | |
|---|---|---|---|---|
| Files | A1 | A3 | A4 | A5 |
| File1 | √ | x | x | x |
| File2 | x | √ | x | x |
| File3 | x | √ | x | x |
| File4 | √ | x | x | x |
| File5 | x | x | √ | x |
| File6 | x | x | x | √ |

√ : access, x : no access,

- : undecided

All staff have the potential to access these files. But they have not had these file access permissions yet.

Table III is the interim table generated by File Permission Decider based on the workload in order to prevent imbalances in workload. In this process, this module receives the Table II, decides the permissions, and updates Table III with Table II. Moreover, the components linked file access permissions with staff information like Table IV, and output it to OverWriter Module.

## V. DISCUSSION

The previous studies mentioned in Section II are for access control systems under normal conditions [1]–[5]. On the other

TABLE IV. OUTPUT OF FILE ACCESS PERMISSIONS

| Files | *Post* | *Name* | *Staff ID* | *IP Address* |
|---|---|---|---|---|
| File1 | Manager | | A1 | 192.0.2.11/24 |
| File2 | Chief | | A3 | 192.0.2.12/24 |
| File3 | Chief | | A3 | 192.0.2.13/24 |
| File4 | Manager | | A1 | 192.0.2.14/24 |
| File5 | Employee | | A4 | 192.0.2.15/24 |
| File6 | Employee | | A5 | 192.0.2.16/24 |

Note ; IP addresses listed in this table are illustrative examples.

hand, our proposed system is beneficial in dealing with any incidents. Moreover, it is useful that the system is introduced to many organizations because the previous system proposed by McGraw in 2010 aimed at military organizations [7]. The proposed system is designed for an on-premises environment in this paper. But it is possible to redesign the system for cloud computing in mind, and all kinds of organizations can adopt the system. The system has not yet been implemented in this paper. But there are potential challenges and limitations. These details are below.

### A. Decrease in resources of the devices

It is less likely to expand cyber attacks from one compromised device, like a springboard attack because the device cannot use files by the proposed system in this paper. But there are possibilities of the reduction of the no affected devices by other attack vectors.

Moreover, when a staff member is attacked and everyone above him is also attacked, the problem arises with Contents Classifier component because it cannot distribute file access permissions that record highly confidential information to his subordinates. Therefore, we should prepare solutions for the management of the number of devices and improve the system.

### B. The staff's past expertise

We proposed a system targeted at staff within a single department. This system utilizes the user expertise that would be required within a department. However, there are employees moving from one different department to another one. When such a movement occurs, the expertise that was required in the previous department should be reflected in user expertise.

### C. Timing of file access permission transfers

In this paper, the administrator who is responsible for the proposed system approves the table sent from OverWriter module. The access permissions are transferred when the module overwrites the file server after approval.

This transfer is most likely to occur while a compromised device is manipulating data. At that time, the device's access right is revoked, making differences between the data stored on file server and edited on the device. Consequently, managing this difference becomes essential because the edited data may contain malware.

To address these issues, we propose storing the edited data in a temporary location such as a quarantine folder. The system should scan the data for malware and retain it for a predetermined period to allow detection of unknown threats. Only after confirming that no problems exist, should it be written back to the original folder as a derived file. This system ensures both consistency and authenticity.

### D. Execution time

Since the system has not yet been implemented, the following issues are anticipated regarding system execution time. There is a possibility that an attacker could edit and save the contents of files using an infected device while the proposed system is running. Especially, this problem is likely to occur when system execution times are long.

### E. Limitations

- Limitations of administrator
  In this paper, the system requires an administrator to review and approve its contents before overwriting the file server with the determined file permissions table. However, he is primarily responsible for managing the proposed system and is likely unfamiliar with the detailed operations within the company. Therefore, the ideal method for this process would be for the victim, who was originally responsible for the tasks, to review and approve the content of the generated table. On the other hand, the challenge is that the victim's computer has been compromised by the cyberattack, making it impossible to facilitate this review.
- On-premise experimental environment
  We assume an experimental organization that manages data in an on-premises environment. An advantage using the environment is that data management can be completed within a company. On the other hand, in order to reduce the efforts or costs of operations in an on-premises environment, many organizations are using the data management system in cloud. Compared with on-premises environments, cloud-based data management systems can cause problems with communication delay. Therefore, it is necessary to evaluate the proposed system under a cloud environment.

## VI. Conclusion And Future Work

We proposed a system for file access management under cyberattack that aims to improve the business continuity in this paper. We expect that the system is effective from the perspective of flexibly changing access permissions under cyber attacks and being adaptable to a variety of organizations. However, we have not implemented the system and conducted verification of the effects. Future work will involve developing the system and conducting experiments to assess the effectiveness, limitations, and robustness of the system under cyber attacks.

## Acknowledgements

This work was supported by JST K Program Grant Number JPMJKP24K3, Japan.

## References

[1] D. D. Downs, J. R. Rub, K. C. Kung, and C. S. Jordan, "Issues in discretionary access control", in *1985 IEEE Symposium on Security and Privacy*, 1985, pp. 208–208. DOI: 10.1109/SP.1985.10014.

[2] J. H. Jafarian, M. Amini, and R. Jalili, "A dynamic mandatory access control model", in *Computer Society of Iran Computer Conference*, Springer, 2008, pp. 862–866.

[3] A. Gabillon, "Web access control strategies", in Jan. 2011, pp. 1368–1371, ISBN: 978-1-4419-5906-5. DOI: 10.1007/978-1-4419-5906-5_664.

[4] D. F. Ferraiolo and D. R. Kuhn, "Role-based access controls", in *Proceedings of the 15th National Computer Security Conference*, Baltimore, MD, USA: National Institute of Standards and Technology (NIST), Oct. 1992, pp. 554–563.

[5] K. Julisch and G. Karjoth, *Method and apparatus for automated assignment of access permissions to users*, US Patent 8,826,455, 2014.

[6] Q. Ni et al., "Privacy-aware role-based access control", *ACM Transactions on Information and System Security (TISSEC)*, vol. 13, no. 3, pp. 1–31, 2010.

[7] R. W. McGraw, "Risk-adaptable access control (RAdAC)", in *Proceedings of the NIST & NSA Privilege Management Workshop*, Paper originally presented September 2009; online PDF accessed June 2025, Gaithersburg, MD, USA: National Institute of Standards and Technology, 2010, pp. 1–10.

[8] A. Shinoda, H. Hasegawa, H. Shimada, Y. Yamaguchi, and H. Takakura, "Feasibility verification of access control system for telecommuting by users reliability calculation", in *Proceedings of the Eighteenth International Conference on Systems and Networks Communications*. International Academy, Research, and Industry Association, Nov. 2023, pp. 16–22.

[9] D. P. Köhler, A. Rausch, T. Biemann, and R. Büchsenschuss, "Expertise and specialization in organizations: A social network analysis", *European Journal of Work and Organizational Psychology*, vol. 34, no. 2, pp. 282–297, 2025.

[10] S. C. Information-technology Promotion Agency Japan (IPA), *Risk analysis sheet: Information security measures guidelines for small and medium-sized enterprises, version 3.1, appendix 7*, Guideline, https://www.ipa.go.jp/security/sme/f55m8k000000587z-att/outline_guidance_risk.pdf, Last accessed: June, 2025, Tokyo, Jul. 2024.

# A Privacy-preserving Video Processing Pipeline

Gábor György Gulyás, Gergely Erdődi
*Vitarex Stúdió Ltd*
Budapest, Hungary
emails: gabor@gulyas.info, erdodi.gergely@vitarex.hu

***Abstract*—We present a modular and scalable video analytics system designed for object detection, face recognition, and multi-camera tracking, with minimal bandwidth consumption and full compatibility with existing video surveillance infrastructure. The architecture emphasizes cost efficiency and regulatory compliance, operating primarily on on-premise deployments to align with constraints imposed by the Artificial Intelligence Act of the European Union and General Data Protection Regulation. After benchmarking a range of object detection, face analysis, and tracking models, we selected the most performant and efficient solutions and orchestrated them using Apache Airflow. The system executes a graph-based processing pipeline that supports parallel, per-camera analytics including people counting, path tracking, heatmap generation, and geofencing. Results are visualized through Apache Superset dashboards, enabling interactive, building-wide situational awareness. By leveraging open source components and a containerized, Kubernetes-compatible deployment model, the solution provides real-time, bandwidth-aware analytics with strong adaptability to diverse operational environments, supporting data-driven decision-making across sectors, such as retail, logistics, and smart infrastructure.**

***Keywords-CCTV; video processing; face recognition; architecture.***

## I. Introduction

The proliferation of video surveillance systems in public and private domains has led to an unprecedented volume of visual data being generated every day. Yet, much of this data remains underutilized, as traditional Closed-Circuit Television (CCTV) infrastructures are designed primarily for passive recording rather than intelligent, real-time interpretation. In response, there is a growing demand across sectors—from retail, logistics and critical infrastructure—for plug-and-play analytics capabilities that can extract actionable insights from video streams without overhauling existing systems for which an example is provided in Figure 1: such systems can log customer activites and map them over the floorplan of the store for providing analytics.

Scalable and bandwidth-efficient video analytics is especially critical in environments where network infrastructure is limited or distributed across multiple physical sites. For organizations managing tens or hundreds of camera feeds, the ability to perform on-device or near-edge inference significantly reduces the load on central servers and minimizes data transfer costs. However, implementing such systems presents numerous challenges.

First, many deployments rely on legacy CCTV hardware that lacks the compute resources necessary for running modern deep learning models. Second, network constraints often prevent continuous high-resolution streaming, which complicates even somewhat real-time inference and analytics. Third, different use cases — such as people counting, heatmap generation, path tracking, geofencing, and facial recognition — require distinct models and processing pipelines, all of which must coexist within the same system. Finally, strict privacy and security regulations, such as the General Data Protection Regulation (GDPR) [1] and the European Union's Artificial Intelligence Act (AI Act) [2], impose legal constraints on how biometric and behavioral data can be processed, stored, and transmitted.

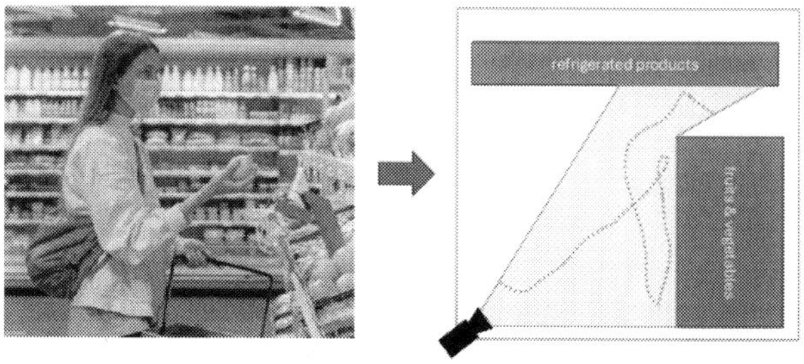


Figure 1. An example how we could use CCTV to map real-world activities into analytics.

To address these challenges, we present a modular and scalable analytics pipeline designed to operate on CPU (Central Processing Unit)- or GPU (Central Processing Unit)-based systems with minimal impact on existing CCTV infrastructure. The system supports multiple analytics tasks concurrently, including object detection, face recognition, activity monitoring, and crowd flow analysis, while maintaining compliance with data protection laws. Our architecture emphasizes deployment flexibility, bandwidth-aware processing, and robust orchestration.

This paper is structured as follows. Section II details the system architecture and deployment design. Then, in Section III, we provide details on the implemented analytics tasks and visualization methods. In Section IV, we discuss our implementation on multi-camera multi-object tracking. Finally, Section V concludes our work.

## II. Architecture Details

Designing the architecture of our video analytics system required balancing multiple constraints, most notably cost-efficiency and regulatory compliance. GPU-enabled cloud infrastructures offer high performance but come with substantial operational costs, making them unsuitable for continuous, large-scale video processing. As such, we prioritized solutions that could run efficiently on CPU-only setups, both to reduce cost and to allow greater deployment flexibility (even though we also used GPU).

Another key architectural decision concerned the mode of operation: whether to process video streams remotely in the cloud or locally on-premise. In addition to cost considerations, legal and ethical concerns — particularly those stemming from the EU AI Act — played a decisive role. Since the Act prohibits biometric identification (such as face recognition) in many public settings unless explicitly authorized, we opted for on-premise pre-processing to ensure compliance and to maintain full control over sensitive data.

Our first step was researching different models and frameworks available for object detection, tracking, and face detection/recognition. We tested a variety of approaches, comparing their accuracy and performance to determine the best fit for our needs. This evaluation included both traditional machine learning techniques and modern deep learning-based models.

Once we identified the most suitable models, we focused on integrating them into a functional pipeline. To efficiently manage workflows, we chose Apache Airflow [3] as our orchestration tool. Airflow allowed us to automate and schedule the processing steps, ensuring seamless data flow and model execution across the system.

### *A. Model Selection*

To select the most suitable components for our video analytics pipeline, we conducted a thorough benchmarking process across four key tasks: object detection, face detection, face recognition, and multi-object tracking. Our evaluation focused on four primary criteria: detection accuracy, inference speed and ease of integration. Additionally, we prioritized models released under permissive licenses such as MIT (created at the Massachusetts Institute of Technology) to ensure freedom for modification, commercial use, and to avoid potential legal or financial restrictions.

**Object Detection**. We evaluated several state-of-the-art object detectors, including YOLOv8 [4] (YOLO in general stands for You Look Only Once), YOLOX [5], EfficientDet [6], and Detectron2 [7]. These models were tested using benchmark datasets, such as COCO (Common Objects in Context) and custom video streams relevant to our target use cases. YOLOv8 provided high accuracy and very fast inference, especially when optimized with TensorRT, with moderate integration effort and an Apache 2.0 license. YOLOX offered similar accuracy, slightly lower inference speed, easier integration, and the same license, making it the preferred choice.

**Face Detection**. For face detection, we compared MediaPipe Face Detection [8], YuNet (a lightweight detector based on NPU-ready backbones, where NPU stands for Neural Processing Units) [9], and MTCNN [10]. MediaPipe was the most resource-efficient and easy to deploy on CPU-based systems. YuNet offered a compelling balance of accuracy and performance, with good hardware compatibility. It was also the fastest and most lightweight, and its compatibility with CUDA hardware acceleration made it the best choice for our use case.

**Face Recognition**. In the face recognition domain, we benchmarked InsightFace [11], SFace [12], and FaceNet [13]. InsightFace, based on ArcFace embeddings, demonstrated superior robustness and accuracy in identity verification tasks, supported by comprehensive pre-trained models and broad platform compatibility. However, due to its restrictive licensing, which does not include an MIT-equivalent license, FaceNet was selected as the preferred alternative. FaceNet offers comparable performance with greater configurability and is distributed under an MIT license, making it more suitable for integration within the system.

**Tracking**. For multi-object tracking, we tested DeepSORT [14] and ByteTrack [15]. While DeepSORT has been widely adopted in academic and commercial applications, ByteTrack showed superior performance in crowded scenes due to its effective association of low-score detections, resulting in fewer identity switches and more stable trajectories. The Kalman filter employed by ByteTrack also provided better speed than DeepSORT.

**Inference Optimization**. To achieve low-latency processing, we integrated NVIDIA TensorRT [16] for inference acceleration. This significantly reduced the runtime of deep models, particularly for object detection and face recognition tasks, enabling high performance even on edge devices with limited resources.

### *B. Architectural Setup*

Our architecture is illustrated in Figure 2, and we discuss its details in the following paragraphs. There are two main components: one is the on-premise preprocessing unit (dealing with computational heavy tasks), and the other is to display results and statistics.

**Pipeline Design and Orchestration**. The system employs Apache Airflow as the central orchestration engine, organizing the entire video analytics pipeline into modular, interdependent tasks through Directed Acyclic Graphs (DAGs). The primary DAG coordinates seven parallel processing tasks including heatmap generation, path tracking, people counting, geofencing, floor plan transformation, activity detection, and face analysis. Each task operates independently, but shares data through Airflow's XCom mechanism, enabling efficient parallel processing while maintaining data consistency across the pipeline. The entire Airflow service runs within a dedicated Docker container [17], while the scheduler operates separately in its own container (within the on-premise device). To support scaling requirements, the system is compatible with Kubernetes and Helm charts, allowing flexible deployment and management in cloud or cluster environments. This setup ensures environment consistency and simplifies deployment, allowing individual components to be modified, scaled, or replaced without impacting the overall system architecture.

**Video Processing and Inference Pipeline**. The video processing architecture employs multithreaded frame sampling with configurable frequency to balance processing speed with tracking accuracy. Each video undergoes systematic frame extraction, where frames are distributed across consumer threads for parallel inference using YOLOX object detection. To optimize performance further, we used OpenCV [18] built with NVIDIA VIDEO CODEC support for hardware-accelerated decoding, which significantly reduces CPU load and improves frame reading speed. The system also maintains separate processing queues with bounded capacity to prevent memory overflow during high-throughput scenarios. Feature extraction operates concurrently with detection, utilizing specialized models for face detection (YuNet), face recognition (FaceNet), and activity estimation when enabled, with results aggregated into tracking histories.

**Camera Integration and Data Sources**. The system operates across multiple network tiers with PostgreSQL [19] serving as the central data repository, while the Airflow scheduler manages task distribution. Video data flows from an ISAPI (Internet Server Application Programming Interface) enabled [20] NVR (Network Video Recorder) through a dedicated scheduler service that continuously monitors recording queues and triggers Airflow processing workflows.

The scheduler service has zone-specific configuration parameters including boundary lines, transformation matrices, and processing frequencies. Video downloads are managed through authenticated sessions with automatic retry mechanisms and status tracking in the database, ensuring reliable data acquisition even under network instability or camera downtime conditions. This system ensures robust error handling and monitoring through transactional safeguards, graceful thread shutdown, automated recovery, and task-level visibility via Airflow, which also provides built-in retry and alert mechanisms.

### C. *System Evaluation*

The current deployment runs on a single machine equipped with an NVIDIA RTX 4060 GPU, 16 GB of RAM, and an Intel Core i5-13400F CPU. Benchmark tests indicate that one hour of Full HD video can be processed in approximately 100 seconds using the GPU, whereas CPU-only processing requires 3.8 hours. At this rate, the system can process up to 72 camera streams per day with GPU acceleration—assuming each camera records 12 hours of footage—compared to 0.5 streams per day using the CPU alone. This throughput is achieved under continuous operation without parallel GPU saturation, providing a reliable baseline for scalability. Further gains can be realized by distributing workloads across multiple GPUs or nodes via the existing Kubernetes-compatible architecture.

Existing open-source tools provide only partial overlaps with this functionality. Kerberos.io is a lightweight, Docker-deployable platform focused primarily on motion detection, with limited AI-based analytics achievable through external integrations. ZoneMinder is designed for recording and basic motion detection, with optional analytics via plugins. In contrast, the proposed pipeline natively integrates object detection, multi-target tracking, optional face recognition, people counting, and heatmap generation (both per-camera and layout-based), while offering a modern analytics-focused web interface and scalable deployment through Docker or Kubernetes.

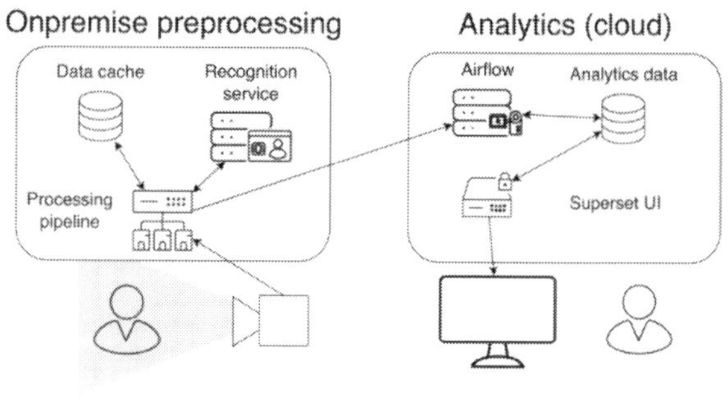


Figure 2. Our architecture setup.

## III. Analytics and Visualization

After setting up Airflow, we needed a way to visualize and interact with the results. For this, we chose Apache Superset, an open source business intelligence tool. Superset enabled us to create interactive dashboards, providing valuable insights from our data and model outputs.

The platform implements a suite of analytic functions (running in the cloud) that transform raw surveillance data into actionable intelligence. **Density analysis** employs Gaussian accumulator matrices [21] with adaptive kernel parameters to generate movement heatmaps that reveal high-traffic zones and pedestrian flow patterns across the monitored environment. **Trajectory analysis** utilizes perspective transformation to create unified coordinate systems that enable cross-camera path tracking, with Bézier curve interpolation providing smooth trajectory visualization that facilitates pattern recognition and anomaly detection.

The system also delivers behavioral analytics through **geofencing** that monitors zone-specific activity and transition events, and **activity recognition** to identify task-specific behaviors, such as object manipulation and stationary activities. (**Demographic analysis** uses facial recognition models to provide age, gender, and ethnicity distribution insights with statistical confidence metrics.)

Visualization outputs encompass multiple analytical modalities including images like **density heatmaps** and **trajectory overlays** with color-coded pathways representing individual movement patterns, and **statistical dashboards** displaying temporal trends through bar charts, line graphs, and occupancy histograms (see example in Figure 3). The platform generates **cumulative analytics** with configurable temporal windows, supporting multi-scale analysis from minute-by-minute monitoring to long-term behavioral pattern identification. Integration with Apache Superset enables interactive dashboard creation with drill-down capabilities, cross-filtering, and automated report generation, providing data-driven insights for operational optimization and security enhancement.

## IV. Multi-Camera Multi-Object Tracking

To further enhance evaluation of tracking data, we incorporated Multi-Camera Multi-Object Tracking (MCMOT),

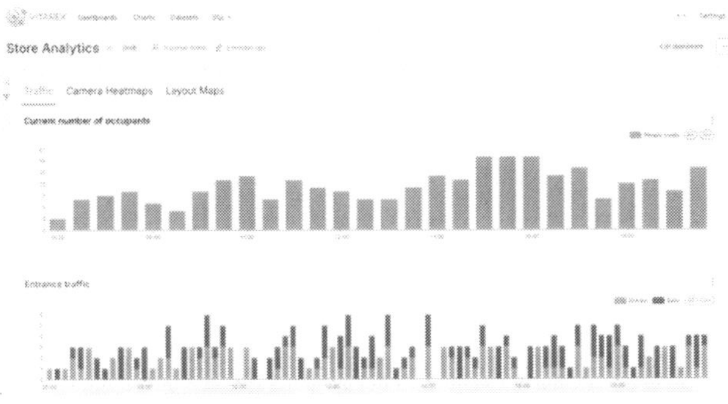


Figure 3. An example from our Apache Superset dashboard.

allowing us to follow individuals across multiple camera feeds. Additionally, we developed a unified layout map that extends per-camera analytics to an entire building. Using projective geometry, we map detections from different cameras onto a real-world floor plan, enabling heatmapping, path tracking, and people counting at a global level. This holistic approach provides a comprehensive view of movement patterns and occupancy trends, further improving surveillance and analytics capabilities.

The tracking system employs **BYTETracker** as the foundation for single-camera object tracking, which maintains temporal consistency through association of detections across consecutive frames. The multi-camera matching system transforms single-camera tracks into trajectory segments that represent a person's movement through the camera's field of view.

**Homography-based mapping to real-world layout.** The system uses perspective transformation matrices to map camera coordinates to a unified layout coordinate system. For each camera, we manually define correspondence points between the camera view and the real-world floor plan. Then, the bottom-center point of each person's bounding box is transformed using the homography matrix [22], providing real-world positioning on the monitored building's floor plan. Then, the tracklet association is done using approximation algorithms.

**Constraint Validation**. The tracking pipeline integrates validation layers to ensure data quality and spatial consistency. Floor mask validation ensures all detections remain within walkable areas, with the help of panoptic segmentation [23] to create a binary mask of the walkable areas and then relocates invalid points to the nearest valid floor position.

## V. Conclusion and Future Work

We presented a scalable, bandwidth-efficient video analytics system that integrates object detection, tracking, and face recognition into existing CCTV infrastructures with minimal overhead. The system leverages open source technologies and is designed for deployment flexibility, supporting both on-premise and cloud-native environments.

Our architecture supports per-camera analytics, such as heatmaps, path tracking, people counting, and geofencing, enabling actionable insights for operational and security decisions. Apache Airflow plays a central role in orchestrating the multi-model pipeline, while model selection was guided by accuracy, performance, and hardware efficiency—particularly under privacy and legal constraints like GDPR and the AI Act.

Future work includes integrating active learning, anomaly detection, and federated training to further enhance performance and compliance across distributed deployments.

## Acknowledgement

The project entitled "GDPR compliant anonymous facial recognition for analytics and improving security", with no. 2021-1.1.4-GYORSÍTÓSÁV-2022-00076 has been implemented with the support provided by the Ministry of Culture and Innovation of Hungary from the National Research, Development and Innovation Fund, financed under the 2021-1.1.4-GYORSÍTÓSÁV funding scheme.

## References

[1] *Regulation (eu) 2016/679 of the european parliament and of the council of 27 april 2016 on the protection of natural persons with regard to the processing of personal data and on the free movement of such data, and repealing directive 95/46/ec (general data protection regulation)*, https://eur-lex.europa.eu/eli/reg/2016/679/oj, Accessed: 2025-04-11, 2016.

[2] *Regulation (eu) 2024/xxxx of the european parliament and of the council laying down harmonised rules on artificial intelligence (artificial intelligence act) and amending certain union legislative acts*, https://eur-lex.europa.eu/legal-content/EN/TXT/?uri=CELEX:52021PC0206, Accessed: 2025-04-11, 2024.

[3] Apache Software Foundation, *Apache airflow: Workflow management platform*, https://airflow.apache.org, Accessed: 2025-06-30, 2023.

[4] G. Jocher et al., "Yolov8: Ultralytics next-generation object detector," *arXiv preprint arXiv:2301.04634*, 2023.

[5] Z. Ge et al., "Yolox: Exceeding yolo series in 2021," *arXiv preprint arXiv:2107.08430*, 2021.

[6] M. Tan, R. Pang, and Q. V. Le, "Efficientdet: Scalable and efficient object detection," *CVPR*, 2020.

[7] Y. Wu et al., "Detectron2," *Facebook AI Research*, 2019, https://github.com/facebookresearch/detectron2.

[8] C. Lugaresi et al., "Mediapipe: A framework for building perception pipelines," *arXiv preprint arXiv:1906.08172*, 2019.

[9] OPPO Research, "Yunet: A fast and accurate face detector," *GitHub repository*, 2022, https://tinyurl.com/fdyunet.

[10] K. Zhang, Z. Zhang, Z. Li, and Y. Qiao, "Joint face detection and alignment using multi-task cascaded convolutional networks," *IEEE Signal Processing Letters*, 2016.

[11] J. Deng et al., "Arcface: Additive angular margin loss for deep face recognition," *CVPR*, 2019.

[12] S. Zhang et al., "Sface: An efficient network for face recognition," *arXiv preprint arXiv:2105.06070*, 2021.

[13] F. Schroff, D. Kalenichenko, and J. Philbin, "Facenet: A unified embedding for face recognition and clustering," *CVPR*, 2015.

[14] N. Wojke, A. Bewley, and D. Paulus, "Simple online and realtime tracking with a deep association metric," *ICIP*, 2017.

[15] Y. Zhang et al., "Bytetrack: Multi-object tracking by associating every detection box," *ECCV*, 2022.

[16] NVIDIA Corporation, *Tensorrt: Nvidia deep learning inference optimizer and runtime*, https://developer.nvidia.com/tensorrt, 2023.

[17] Docker Inc., *Docker: Empowering app development for developers*, https://www.docker.com, Accessed: 2025-06-30, 2023.

[18] OpenCV Contributors, *Opencv: Open source computer vision library*, https://opencv.org, Accessed: 2025-06-30, 2023.

[19] PostgreSQL Global Development Group, *Postgresql: The world's most advanced open source relational database*, https://www.postgresql.org, Accessed: 2025-06-30, 2023.

[20] Hikvision Digital Technology Co., Ltd, *Isapi protocol specification*, https://www.hikvision.com, Accessed: 2025-06-30, 2023.

[21] B. Zhou, Y. Tang, and X. Wang, "Understanding crowd behaviors using dynamic textures and statistical analysis," *IEEE Transactions on Pattern Analysis and Machine Intelligence*, vol. 34, no. 5, pp. 895–908, 2011. DOI: 10.1109/TPAMI.2011.176.

[22] R. Hartley and A. Zisserman, *Multiple View Geometry in Computer Vision*. Cambridge university press, 2004.

[23] A. Kirillov, K. He, R. Girshick, C. Rother, and P. Dollár, "Panoptic segmentation," in *CVPR*, 2019, pp. 9404–9413.

# Contributions to Methodologies to Improve Sensor Data Quality of Cyber Physical Production Systems Through Digitalisation: A Use Case Approach

Martin Zinner*, Hajo Wiemer*, Kim Feldhoff*, Peter Meschke*, and Steffen Ihlenfeldt*§
*Technische Universität Dresden
Institute of Mechatronic Engineering (IMD); Chair of Machine Tools Development and Adaptive Controls (LWM)
01062 Dresden, Germany
§Fraunhofer Institute for Machine Tools and Forming Technology (IWU)
01062 Dresden, Germany
Email: {martin.zinner1, hajo.wiemer, kim.feldhoff, peter.meschke, steffen.ihlenfeldt}@tu-dresden.de

***Abstract*—Cyber Physical Production Systems (CPPS) depend significantly on high-quality sensor data to function optimally, make decisions in real-time, and perform predictive maintenance inter alia. Nevertheless, the quality of sensor data in industrial settings is often affected by various factors such as environmental interference, hardware wear and tear, calibration drift, and intricate system interactions. This study introduces innovative methods to improve sensor data quality in CPPS through systematic digitalization strategies. By employing a use case methodology, we explore real-world production scenarios to pinpoint common data quality challenges and devise specific solutions. Our strategy integrates signal processing techniques, algorithms for detecting anomalies to establish robust frameworks for data validation and correction. The proposed methods offer practical, scalable solutions that can be adapted to various production environments, thereby enhancing the reliability and efficiency of cyber physical manufacturing systems. To illustrate the feasibility of our approach, we utilise the case study of a test bed.**

***Keywords*-Failure analysis; Sensor data quality; Sensor data error detection.**

## I. INTRODUCTION

This section analyses the motivation, challenges, aims, research questions and contributions of this study. The objective of our study was to improve the quality of Cyber Physical Production Systems (CCPS) data through digitalisation by implementing a methodology to improve the quality of sensor data [1]. CPPSs consist of self-governing and collaborative components and subsystems. These elements are interconnected based on contextual factors, spanning all production levels. The integration extends from individual processes and machinery to comprehensive production and logistics networks [2].

For the sake of simplicity, within this study, we use the term "real-time", since it is used exhaustively in the scientific and technical literature, but it should be understood that we are always referring to "near real-time". To avoid confusion, the term "near real-time" implies that the required latency is not guaranteed, as in real-time systems, but only envisaged. In simple terms, for real-time systems, the latency of the system is part of its functional correctness; a near real-time system will function correctly if the required latency is inadvertently not achieved.

### A. Motivation

In the realm of modern CPPS, there is an increasing dependence on extensive sensor networks to continuously track essential process parameters, equipment condition, and product quality. Despite this, ensuring high-quality sensor data remains a significant challenge that affects manufacturing efficiency, product uniformity, and operational safety. Inadequate sensor data quality can result in false alarms, undetected faults, inefficient process control, and ultimately higher production costs and diminished competitiveness.

Traditional methods for sensor validation often involve manual checks, statistical limits, or basic redundancy checks, which fall short in addressing the complexity and scale of contemporary production settings. These conventional techniques often miss subtle sensor degradation, issues with cross-sensor correlations, or context-specific anomalies that arise in dynamic manufacturing processes. Moreover, current solutions typically focus on sensor quality in isolation, neglecting the broader digital infrastructure and data processing workflows that define Industry 4.0 environments [3].

The incorporation of advanced digital technologies—such as machine learning, edge computing, and intelligent data processing—offers unprecedented opportunities to improve sensor data quality assessment and management. By developing systematic approaches that utilize digitalization capabilities, manufacturers can establish more robust, scalable, and adaptive sensor quality assurance systems. This research highlights the urgent need for comprehensive, digitalization-enabled strategies that can automatically identify, categorize, and address sensor data quality issues while seamlessly integrating with existing CPPS frameworks [4]–[6].

The practical validation of these methodologies through real-world applications demonstrates their relevance and effectiveness, providing manufacturers with actionable frameworks to enhance sensor reliability and, consequently, the overall performance of production systems.

### B. Challenges

The adoption of digitalization-driven methods for enhancing sensor data quality in CPPS settings introduces numerous technical and practical hurdles that need to be overcome for effective implementation. Contemporary production sites utilize a wide array of sensor technologies from various manufacturers, each featuring unique communication protocols, sampling rates, data formats, and quality attributes. Crafting unified quality assessment strategies that can effectively manage this diversity while ensuring precision across different sensor types is a challenging task.

CPPS applications require immediate evaluation of sensor data quality to avert defective production or equipment damage. However, advanced quality assessment algorithms often demand substantial computational resources, leading to a conflict between processing complexity and the need for real-time performance, especially in resource-limited edge computing settings [7].

As sensor networks expand in size and complexity, maintaining consistent quality assessment performance while managing computational demands, communication bandwidth, and system maintenance requirements becomes increasingly challenging, particularly for large-scale industrial applications.

### C. Aim

The main goal of this study is to create and validate comprehensive methods that utilize digitalization technologies to systematically enhance sensor data quality in CPPS. This research specifically aims to fulfill the following objectives:

Design and implement practical solutions capable of evaluating sensor quality in real-time while adhering to the strict performance standards of industrial production settings. This involves creating efficient algorithms suitable for edge computing platforms and resource-limited operational conditions.

Validate the practical applicability and effectiveness of the proposed methods through detailed case studies in actual production environments. The Suspension Motion Simulator case study serves as the main validation platform to assess algorithm performance, detection accuracy, and operational feasibility.

Offer clear guidelines and implementation strategies that allow manufacturers to incorporate these digitalization-enabled quality improvement methods into existing CPPS infrastructures with minimal disruption to ongoing operations.

### D. Contribution

This study introduces several innovative advancements in managing sensor data quality within CPPS through digitalization: Development and validation of a practical strategy for real-time sensor quality assessment in production settings using optimized algorithms suitable for edge computing platforms.

Establishment of a systematic approach for validating sensor quality improvement methods through controlled industrial case studies. The Suspension Motion Simulator implementation showcases the practical applicability of the proposed methods and provides measurable performance metrics for evaluation.

Contribution of a modular, scalable approach adaptable across different production scales and sensor network complexities, from single-machine implementations to facility-wide deployments. These contributions collectively enhance the state-of-the-art in sensor data quality management for modern manufacturing systems and offer practical tools for improving production reliability through digitalization technologies.

### E. Paper organisation

The structure of this paper is outlined as follows. An overview of relevant existing research pertaining to the described problem is provided in Section II. A detailed description of the strategy is presented in Section III, whereas Section IV demonstrates the feasibility of this strategy through an example. The presentation of the main results and discussions based on these results constitute the content of Section V. Finally, Section VI summarises this contribution and draws perspectives for future work.

## II. Related work

Recent studies in sensor data quality management for CPPS have concentrated on tackling essential calibration issues and creating digitalization-driven solutions for industrial settings [8].

The phenomenon of sensor drift has been thoroughly investigated across various sensor technologies [9] illustrated that zero-point drift has a substantial impact on measurement precision in mechanical spectroscopy applications, while [10] pinpointed bulk equilibration effects as the main reason for baseline drift in metal oxide gas sensors. The detailed analysis by [11] showed that environmental factors, wear-and-tear, and manufacturing inconsistencies lead to gradual sensor deterioration, with drift rates differing significantly among sensor types and operating conditions. Electrochemical sensor systems display unique drift characteristics, as evidenced in [12], where both exponential sensitivity decline and linear baseline shifts occur concurrently. Temperature-induced drift mechanisms have been particularly well-documented, with [13] demonstrating that thermal expansion coefficients and bridge circuit asymmetries are key contributors to zero-point errors in pressure sensors.

The use of machine learning techniques for assessing sensor quality has garnered considerable interest. [11] effectively applied isolation forest algorithms for real-time drift detection, achieving early recognition of sensor degradation patterns. Multi-sensor array strategies using orthogonal signal correction have been developed by [14], showing effective drift compensation through baseline manipulation and partial least squares regression. Advanced compensation methods incorporating neural networks and polynomial fitting have been explored by [15], indicating that radial basis function networks can accurately model complex non-linear temperature relationships in sensor systems. These methods allow for automatic calibration adjustments without the need for frequent manual intervention.

Practical deployment considerations have been addressed through various industrial case studies. [16] developed federated learning approaches for electronic nose systems, facilitating cross-facility knowledge sharing while preserving data privacy. The research demonstrates that multivariate calibration models can be effectively updated using distributed sensor networks without compromising proprietary information. Temperature drift compensation strategies have been validated in industrial settings, with [17] providing quantitative methods for calculating zero and sensitivity drift coefficients. These strategies enable predictive maintenance scheduling and reduce the need for frequent calibration in production environments.

While existing research tackles individual aspects of sensor quality management, comprehensive frameworks that integrate real-time detection, automated compensation, and industrial-scale deployment are still limited, see [18] for an example of heterogeneous networks. Designing heterogeneous sensor networks presents the challenge of ensuring that sensors can collaborate effectively despite their differences. This involves creating protocols and algorithms capable of managing data flow, maintaining data quality, and optimizing energy use, etc. A generic model is developed [19], yet it is recognized that current industrial monitoring relies on basic Statistical Process Control limits. Most current approaches focus on single sensor types or specific drift mechanisms, lacking the comprehensive methodology needed for diverse CPPS environments. This research addresses these gaps by developing an integrated digitalization framework that combines multiple quality assessment techniques with practical validation through industrial use cases.

## III. STRATEGY

In this section, we explicitly delineate the focus of the underlying investigation and outline a strategy that can be employed to achieve these goals. This is in relation to the detailed use case study presented in Section IV. We succintly present a list of possible sensor outlier and analyze as illustrative the calibration related outliers [19]–[35]. This list includes crucial types, but it is not comprehensive.

- **Sensor Outliers and Common Causes:**
  - **Calibration-Related Outliers:**
    - Gradual drift - Over time, sensors become less accurate due to factors like aging components, temperature fluctuations, or material wear.
    - Baseline shift - The initial reading changes, resulting in all measurements being consistently offset by a fixed amount.
    - Sensitivity errors - Changes in the sensor's sensitivity lead to readings that are consistently too high or too low by a certain percentage.
    - Non-linear response - The sensor's response becomes non-linear throughout its range, leading to inaccuracies at specific measurement points.
  - **Environmental Outliers:**
    - Impact of temperature - Extreme heat or cold leading to sensor readings deviating from standard ranges.
    - Humidity disruption - Moisture influencing electrical sensors or optical parts.
    - Electromagnetic interference (EMI) - Radio waves or electrical fields distorting sensor signals.
    - Vibration-induced noise - Mechanical vibrations causing inaccurate readings in accelerometers or pressure sensors.
  - **Physical Damage or Contamination:**
    - Fouling - Accumulation of dust, oil, or chemicals on sensor surfaces impacting optical or chemical sensors.
    - Corrosion - Metal components in pH sensors or electrochemical devices undergoing oxidation.
    - Physical obstruction - Items obstructing ultrasonic or optical sensors.
    - Wire degradation - Damaged or corroded connections leading to sporadic readings.
  - **Installation and Mechanical Issues:**
    - Installation issues - Loose sensors causing vibration disturbances or positional inaccuracies, loose connections, broken cables, etc.
    - Thermal expansion - Variations in temperature leading to mechanical stress and alterations in measurements.
    - Pressure seal failures - In pressure sensors, resulting in faulty atmospheric compensation.
  - **Electronic and Signal Processing Outliers:**
    - Errors in converting analog signals to digital - Issues like bit flips or quantization problems during digitization.
    - Fluctuations in power supply - Variations in voltage that impact sensor excitation and output.
    - Ground loops - Signal corruption due to electrical noise from improper grounding.
    - Crosstalk in multiplexers - In systems with multiple channels, signals interfering between channels.
- **Advanced Outlier Categories:**
  - **Communication and Data Transmission Issues:**
    - Packet loss - Missing data points in wireless sensor networks creating gaps or interpolation errors.
    - Timing synchronization errors - Clock drift causing timestamp misalignment in multi-sensor systems.
    - Protocol errors - Communication protocol failures leading to corrupted or duplicated readings.
    - Buffer overflow - Data acquisition systems dropping samples during high-rate collection.
    - Performance problems with data transfer - network too slow or computing power (CPU overloaded)
  - **Software and Firmware Outliers:**
    - Errors in floating-point precision - Accumulation of rounding mistakes during computations.
    - Firmware issues - Software malfunctions leading to consistent errors or sporadic incorrect readings.
    - Memory corruption - RAM faults impacting stored calibration data or processing algorithms.
    - Stack overflow - Program failures causing sensors to produce default or erroneous values.
  - **Operational Context Outliers:**

* Saturation - Occurs when sensors hit their maximum measurement capacity, leading to clipping or wrapping around.
* Hysteresis effects - Sensor outputs influenced by previous measurement history.
* Settling time violations - Taking sensor readings before they have stabilized following changes in input.
* Sample rate aliasing - Insufficient sampling of rapidly changing signals, resulting in misleading low-frequency content.

Failure Mode and Effects Analysis (FMEA) methodologies present several significant benefits for ensuring the quality of sensor data. By identifying potential sensor failure modes before they happen, FMEA allows for preventive actions instead of reactive ones. It ensures thorough coverage by investigating all possible sensor failure scenarios, such as drift, calibration errors, environmental interference, and physical damage. Additionally, it offers a data-driven framework to prioritize which sensor quality issues need immediate attention. In dynamic manufacturing settings, FMEA is most effective when integrated with real-time monitoring and Artificial Intelligence (AI)-based anomaly detection systems [36].

In the following, as an example, we give some Python and R utilities that can be used to address calibration related outliers [37]–[42]:

Python Tools:

- scipy.optimize.least_squares() - Utilized for robust calibration fitting that includes outlier management
- sklearn.linear_model.RANSACRegressor() - Employed for calibration regression that is resistant to outliers.
- scipy.stats.zscore() - Applied for detecting statistical outliers in calibration datasets.

R Tools:

- MASS::rlm() - Used for fitting robust linear models in calibration.
- robustbase::lmrob() - Implemented for robust regression with outlier identification.
- RobustCalibration package - Designed for robust Bayesian calibration techniques.
- car::outlierTest() - Utilized for statistical testing of outliers in calibration models.

## IV. Use case

This section demonstrates the practical application of the solution concept described in Section III. The concept was implemented and validated using the "Suspension Motion Simulator" (SMS) case study at the Institute for Automotive Engineering, Technische Universität Dresden, Germany (Figure 1), see [43]. The progressive digitalization of CPPS establishes the foundation for AI-driven approaches, including data mining and predictive analytics. Within this context, the case study aimed to develop a functional strategy for identifying sensor data errors on the simulator in real-time. The following key areas were explored:

- Outlining the test bench setup, including integrated sensors and their roles in various testing tasks.
- Examining relevant measurement chains to identify potential error influences and their impact on signal curves.
- Investigating algorithms for identifying and mitigating common data quality issues caused by test bench malfunctions and environmental factors.
- Demonstrating error detection and categorization in data using MATLAB or a similar development tool.

The resulting algorithm enables immediate diagnosis of data quality issues during the measurement process. The aim is to create a computer model that is as accurate as possible, thereby enabling simulation.

Many measurement data sets contain errors and other anomalies. However, these must be error-free for machine learning applications, a context-sensitive analysis is desirable. Errors within data sets can lead to mistakes in analysis, resulting in misinterpretations within the given context and, eventually, incorrect decisions. This may cause defects in product quality or harm the CPPS. Ultimately, this poses a major challenge to the adoption of ML in production due to the lack of trust in AI. It is therefore necessary to detect and eliminate errors. If this is not possible, the data set must be excluded and regenerated. In most cases, however, this is not possible because the vehicles can only be on the test bench for a limited time. To solve this problem, it is necessary to detect errors as quickly as possible and repeat the measurements. In order to obtain a sufficiently large error-free data set, old measurement data must also be checked again for accuracy and merged with newly generated measurement data.

The script developed in the course of this work and the algorithm behind it should make a major contribution to this. By quickly detecting a selection of errors, it should be possible to repeat the measurements on the same day, thereby relieving the pressure on the production team and customers and saving time and money. In addition, it should enable the creation of an error-free database for further use with machine learning.

### A. *Test bench setup*

The test bench, which was supplied by the manufacturer MTS Systems (MTS), 2021 , is supplemented by additional systems installed by the chair. The test bench is an integral component of the parameterisation line under development at the vehicle technology test centre, German: Fahrzeugtechnisches Versuchszentrum (FVZ). It will eventually facilitate the largely automated determination of a vehicle's parameters. The objective is to develop a highly precise computer model to enable simulation. The test bench can be divided into four basic subsystems, which consist of further complex systems and are explained below.

The initial subsystem is the test bench itself, which is supported by a substantial foundation designed to dampen vibrations using three air springs positioned at its corners. Steel rails cover the foundation's base, enabling the attachment of various systems. The most significant system affixed in this manner is the test bench. Positioned atop this are two

Figure 1. Main table of the test bench and its four electromagnets [43]. Four powerful electromagnets are placed on the main table, to which the car sill or a suitable adapter can be clamped.

tables, both of which can be vertically adjusted to fit vehicles of varying sizes. The main table is equipped with four strong electromagnets, allowing for the clamping of a car's sill or an appropriate adapter (refer to Figure 1).

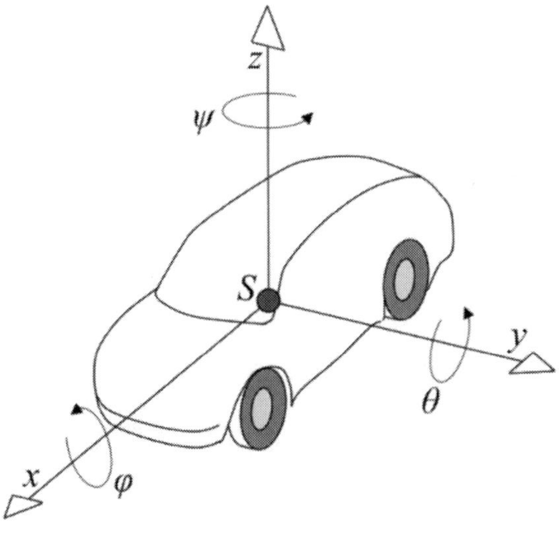


Figure 2. Vehicle coordinate system according to DIN 70000. In this figure, $\varphi$ represents the roll angle, $\theta$ indicates the pitch angle, and the yaw angle $\psi$ is also shown [43].

When the hydraulics are activated, the stamps can apply a force of up to 20,000 N and operate swiftly, necessitating careful handling. The platforms are designated as Right Front (RF) on the right side in the direction of travel and Left Front (LF) on the left side. Figure 2 illustrates a sketch of the test bench coordinate system. In this figure, $\varphi$ represents the roll angle, $\theta$ indicates the pitch angle, and the yaw angle $\psi$ is also shown. The tyre's coordinate system aligns with the vehicle's coordinate system and originates at the center of the rim.

The test bench is operated by a controller, which is linked to a computer located in a separate room for safety purposes. This computer hosts a virtual machine that runs the control software provided by MTS.

This management approach, as specified by the manufacturer, ensures the software operates reliably across various operating systems. Additionally, the program allows for the control of different platforms.

Once the set-up procedure is complete, the vehicle is hoisted onto the test bench using a crane. This involves sliding four claws beneath the car. On the test bench, the vehicle is secured.The set-up process includes installing measurement equipment like potentiometers, cable gauges, and other instruments. Additionally, the vehicle's weight and dimensions are recorded. This data is crucial for accurately setting up the vehicle on the test bench.

The Aramis SRX optical measurement system, see Figure 3 created by GOM, a company that specializes in optical measurement technology (GOM, 2021), is installed on the test bench. It is positioned on two platforms, one on each side of the bench, allowing for the detection of even the slightest movements of the chassis or rims.

Figure 3. IT concept of the "Aramis SRX optical measuring system" test stand [43].

For this purpose, reflection points are affixed to the relevant assembly and logged into the software. This setup permits the measurement of movements relative to the primary coordinate system, as illustrated in Figure 2, located at the vehicle's center. During recording, these points are illuminated with blue light to facilitate tracking. The reflection points bounce back this light, allowing each point to be distinctly recognized.

Various tests can be carried out on the test bench. In most cases, however, the so-called standard tests are carried out. These refer to nine basic test types, which are listed in the following Table I.

Table I offers a concise summary of the fundamental tests. Numerous variations and specific instances exist for each of these standard test scenarios. The table includes the tests that

TABLE I. OVERVIEW OF THE INDIVIDUAL STANDARD TESTS ON THE TEST BENCH

| Test code | Description |
|---|---|
| T01 | Vertical test |
| T02 | Roll test |
| T03 a.) | Lateral compliance test aiding |
| T03 b.) | Lateral compliance tests opposing |
| T04 | Longitudinal Braking Compliance Test |
| T05 | Longitudinal Acceleration Compliance Test |
| T06 a.) | Align Torque Compliance Aiding |
| T06 b.) | Aligning Torque Compliance Opposing |
| T07 | Steering Ratio Tests |
| T08 | Cornering Test |
| T09 | Longitudinal Compliance Test |

are most frequently conducted. Additionally, there is a test definition from MTS that outlines various tests, their functions, and other pertinent parameters (MTS Systems, 2020). These serve as the standard for 'Kinematics and Compliance' test benches. The tests employed by the test bench team closely resemble or are derived from these.

There are numerous other testing scenarios that can be explored. For instance, white noise, which produces a random signal with a particular amplitude and frequency, can be utilized. Additionally, one can create a completely self-generated signal and store it for future playback. This capability allows for any dynamic excitation within the operational limits of the test bench. It also enables the simulation of actual road conditions to identify the source of a noise. However, generating such a signal demands significant effort.

During the initial phase of the evaluation, a mat file is generated from the measurement data. This task is accomplished using a Matlab script developed by the test bench team. The script consolidates the different files from both the test bench and the Aramis system into a unified file. Consequently, the mat file encompasses all the necessary data for evaluation. Following this, another script is employed to plot the data, resulting in various diagrams that depict the measurement data over time. These diagrams are instrumental in evaluating the quality of the measurement data.

During the second phase, the data undergoes verification. Initially, it is determined whether all measurement data channels are included or if the signal from either the right or left side of the test bench is absent in a diagram. If everything is in order, the next step involves evaluating the quality of the measurement data, focusing on the noise levels across different channels. Should one channel exhibit significantly more noise than the others, the measurement must be redone. Subsequently, the measurement plan is reviewed to confirm that all documented forces and positions have been achieved. If discrepancies are found, they may have arisen from errors in inputting boundary data or during the test bench's execution. Following this, the reproducibility of the graphs is assessed by examining the hysteresis, which should generally follow similar trajectories. The final step in data verification involves checking for errors, such as anomalies like jumps or missing values. If the graphs display no unacceptable jumps in measured values and the lines are mostly continuous, the measurement data is considered acceptable. Once all these checks are completed, a decision can be made on whether the measurement needs to be repeated or if it is suitable for further analysis.

When examining a system as intricate as a test bench, a methodical approach is crucial. To address all elements thoroughly and impartially, it is important to first identify the main issues, which will serve as a foundation for subsequent analysis. The next chapter outlines the techniques employed for this purpose.

To evaluate the test bench, a comprehensive examination of the entire setup was conducted. The primary inquiry was: 'What subsystems are identifiable within the complete test bench, and how can these be effectively reduced to the essential components?' To address this, a mind map was developed, and once all systems were documented, efforts were made to discern a pattern. This approach was intended to ensure that the test bench analysis was thorough and comprehensible. The subsystems identified are:

- Suspension motion simulator
- Hydraulic unit
- Test specimen
- Crane
- Aramis SRX

As the work progressed, the individual subsystems and their roles were analyzed. The suspension motion simulator was the most detailed among them. To clearly outline all its functions, an additional breakdown of the SMS was required. The emphasis was on its operation and design, potential configurations, and internal data logging. Furthermore, the possibility of integrating other measuring devices, such as potentiometers, with the test bench was also explored.

Initially, the chosen errors were organized in a logical sequence for verification. It is illogical to assess different noise levels when entire channels are absent or filled with empty values. Consequently, it was determined that the data's completeness should be verified first, followed by the functions that necessitate complete measurement data, such as noise analysis.

Subsequently, the measurement data underwent a thorough review. To identify the algorithm's error, it was necessary to find a logical or mathematical method for detection. This required a detailed analysis of the channel curves and the identification of an appropriate Matlab function.

Utilizing name lists guarantees easy scalability, allowing for the addition of new channels in the future as needed. The program will then verify these additions. To determine if the function accurately identifies errors, faulty data records are accessed, and an additional method known as error injection is employed. This involves manually introducing the desired anomalies into the measurement data. For instance, in jump detection, an extra jump was artificially created to observe how the program responds in such scenarios.

*B. Important aspects for measurement data quality*

To date, adherence to these criteria in the Suspension Motion Simulator has been maintained through manual oversight of the measurement data. The newly developed algorithm aims to autonomously verify the criteria of completeness and correctness, paving the way for future automated verification and assessment of measurement data, with the ultimate goal of integrating machine learning into the test bench.

*C. Error detection and categorisation in measurement data*

In a complex system like the Suspension Motion Simulator, various errors can arise. To create a Matlab script – the simulation requires a Matlab file, hence Matlab was chosen for identifying the errors – capable of identifying these errors and notifying the responsible engineer, a thorough understanding of each specific error is essential. This chapter outlines the errors that have been encountered, explores methods for detecting them, and examines the design and operation of the algorithm that has been developed.

Numerous errors can arise with the suspension motion simulator. Some of these errors occur simultaneously, while others happen independently. A concise summary of the errors encountered so far is presented in Table II. Errors that are the focus of this paper are explained in more detail below.

TABLE II. THIS TABLE CONTAINS ERRORS THAT HAVE OCCURRED DURING TEST BENCH OPERATION TO DATE.

| Error | Source | Description | Freq. |
|---|---|---|---|
| Missing channels | GOM | Entire channels missing from measurement data | Rare |
| Missing points | GOM | Measurement points missing | Rare |
| Incorrect data | GOM | Malfunction in Aramis file | Rare |
| Jumps | GOM | Data jumps implausibly | Very rare |
| Overload | SMS | Force/torque exceeded, emergency stop | Frequent |
| Controller error | SMS | Controller error causes problems | Very rare |
| Irregular graph | Hydraulic | Oil viscosity changes due to heating failure | Very rare |
| Overheatin; | Hydraulic | Oil too warm, cooling unable to maintain temp | Very rare |

If Aramis captures entirely inaccurate measurement data, the issue typically lies within the loaded file. Before initiating a measurement, it is essential to input and group the marked individual points into the system. Additionally, distances between various coordinate systems can be established. Contours, such as a steamer on the front axle, can also be scanned at different locations and subsequently saved as cylinders in the file. Occasionally, these objects might be rotated in space, deviating from their original positions, leading to erroneous measurement data. To safeguard the test bench from damage, it is equipped with an emergency shut-off mechanism that activates when specific distance or force thresholds are surpassed. If the forces become excessive, the tire might slip on the corundum of the measuring platforms, reaching an unacceptable force or distance value. Furthermore, if the steering wheel is obstructed by a steering wheel lock, the existing torque around the Z-axis (refer to Figure 2) can become so substantial that it causes slippage. This also results in unacceptable values, prompting the test bench to enter emergency shutdown mode. During an emergency shutdown, the measurement process is halted, and the hydraulics are deactivated.

A highly uncommon error is initiated by the controller, which then assumes control of the test bench. Should a malfunction occur, issues may arise, such as when employing the 'platforms away from wheels' script. In such instances, the test bench becomes unresponsive and powers down. Additionally, if the hydraulic oil is not at the appropriate temperature, complications can ensue. Typically, a heater within the hydraulic unit regulates the temperature. However, if the necessary sensor malfunctions, emergency mode must be activated. In this mode, the oil is warmed solely by the test bench's movement. A temperature that is too low can cause a wave-like pattern in a graph that would otherwise be sinusoidal. Conversely, if the hydraulic oil becomes excessively warm, issues will also occur. Should the hydraulic unit's cooling system fail to provide adequate power, it will shut down, leading all test benches to enter emergency shutdown. This situation has been a rare occurrence in the past.

On the test bench, there are several distinct measuring chains, each comprising various stations where measurement data is generated, processed, or transmitted. This reseach focuses solely on the optical measuring system chain, as the specific errors identified are produced by the Aramis SRX system.

Next measurement data is conveyed through three cables located at the rear of the measuring bar. This data is subsequently processed using the manufacturer's software, resulting in the creation of a file that contains the measurement data. Initially, this file is temporarily saved on the GOM PC's hard drive before being transferred to the network drive. To accomplish this, the data must be retransmitted via an Ethernet cable linked to the GOM PC.

Finally, the data is stored on the network drive, ensuring that all computers can access and further process the measurement data.

Another crucial factor is interference, which pertains to influences that could damage or distort the measurement data. Errors are particularly likely during data transmission through the cables, which have connectors at each end that can present additional risks if mishandled. Examples include cable breaks that render data transmission impossible, and the breakage of one or more of the delicate pins in the connectors, which can also hinder accurate data transmission. Additionally, strong magnetic fields can disrupt the transmission of measurement data.

In this study, a limited number of errors from the test bench were selected. From these, an appropriate algorithm has been developed to identify these anomalies and promptly repeat the related measurements. To create and ultimately test this algorithm, erroneous measurement data is necessary, which was supplied by the test bench team. All evaluated errors stemmed from malfunctions of the Aramis-SRX.

There are several possible causes for this issue. One possibility is a failure in the data transfer from Aramis to the control computer in the control room, resulting in the data being unavailable. Another scenario could be an error in the naming of individual channels on the Aramis computer. If the script intended to create the MAT file is supposed to generate it from the tables sent, it may not find a channel with the specified name and leave it blank.

To detect such missing entries, one method is to compare the actual name with a pre-established list of target names. If the name is found, the program can proceed. If not, corrective actions must be taken.

A common issue that can arise is the absence of data points, which manifest as voids in the graph and, if too numerous, can make the measurement invalid.

Figure 4 serves as an illustration of this problem. A detailed examination of the wheel center's displacement diagram in the X direction over time reveals missing points for the FL (front left). This issue persists in the diagram showing displacement relative to force in the X direction over time, it is noticeable that some points are missing for FL (front left). This is also reflected in the diagram showing the displacement over the force in the X direction. These voids are typically produced by the Aramis system when one or more measurement points are no longer detected. This can be caused by a software glitch, damage to the reflective surfaces of the points, or vehicle movement due to input from the test bench. Such gaps may also occur during the creation of the MAT file when synchronization or upsampling is conducted, leading to unfeasible operations during this process, and Matlab inserts 'NaN' values at these locations.

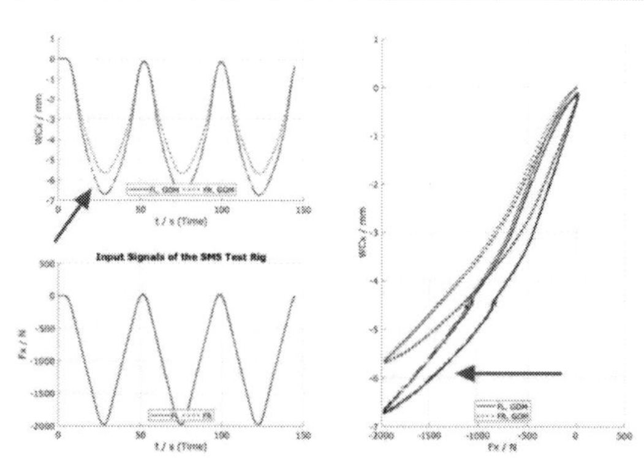


Figure 4. Plotted measurement data from a T04 with errors in the front left data. On closer inspection of the diagram showing the wheel centre displacement in the X direction over time.

There are several methods to identify and correct such errors, see the following explanations. An attempt was made to process the measurement data using both high-pass and low-pass filters. However, because the jumps did not occur at a specific frequency, this approach was ineffective. A median filter was also applied, but it failed to deliver the desired results with the substantial jumps observed here. Consequently, the idea of filtering the measurement data to eliminate jumps was abandoned. Another method to detect the jumps is to remove points that deviate from the mean value by a certain percentage. Additionally, there is the option of calculating the difference between consecutive points and setting a threshold value for this.

An additional error that may arise pertains to the noise levels in the various measurement channels. The noise levels of the signals on the left and right sides differ. This discrepancy can result from external factors during data transmission or from inaccuracies in recording the measurement data. Figure 5 illustrates an example of this error pattern. In the top left diagram, which depicts the wheel center displacement in the Y direction over time, the left side exhibits a highly noisy signal. Conversely, the right side's signal is much clearer. This difference is also apparent in the diagram showing the wheel center displacement in the Y direction over force, where a significantly larger amplitude is noticeable on the vehicle's left side.

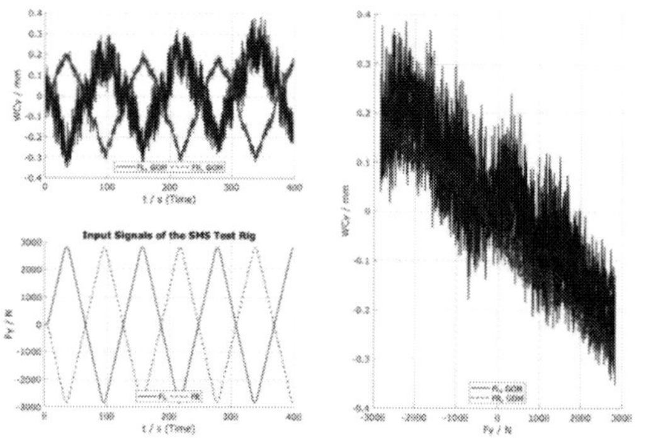


Figure 5. Plotted measurement data from a T03 with channels of varying noise levels for wheel centre displacement in the Z direction.

To assess the noise levels in the measurement data, Fourier analysis is employed. This technique allows for the plotting of amplitude against frequency, enabling insights into the various components. By comparing the data obtained through this method, it becomes evident whether the channels on the left and right sides exhibit different noise levels.

The algorithm's first task is to verify completeness, ensuring all channels are present and the measurement data is free of NaN values (erroneous values). The program should terminate if a channel is absent or if the number of missing values surpasses a certain threshold. Although checking for NaN values was initially intended as a separate step, it was found more practical to incorporate it into the first step during programming. In the second step, the measurement data is examined for jumps, which are values so implausible that they are considered measurement errors.

Such measurements can skew the overall outcome and need to be identified or, if necessary, eliminated. If this cannot be done, the measurement should be conducted again. In the subsequent step, the data is examined to assess the level of noise and to check for significant discrepancies in this aspect. If the LF side channel is considerably noisier than the RF side, the measurement should be redone.

As per the diagram, the first requirement is the generated MAT file. This file, along with structures, such as GOM, Bank GOM, and Bank MTS, among others, is imported by the main program, as they are essential for the verification process. Subsequently, a pre-existing list that includes all approved names for the various GOM channels is loaded. The significant advantage of this list is its ability to be updated at any time without necessitating code modifications. Therefore, if a new channel needs to be added or a name change is required in the future, it can be done with minimal effort.

### *D. Mathematical background of the individual methods*

The Fourier analysis tool is essential for identifying the different frequencies present in the noise. However, the exact method for making the comparison still needs to be developed. The next section aims to explain the approaches that will be implemented in the program code. Initially, a channel was selected from the measurement data that exhibited a significant noise difference between the left and right sides. This data represented the wheel center's displacement in the X direction over time. It was thoroughly analyzed, and a Fourier analysis was conducted to identify the various dominant frequency components and their amplitudes.

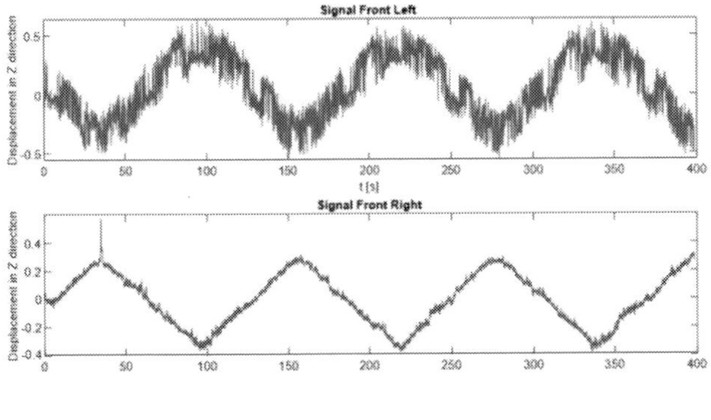


Figure 6. Signal from the left and right sides with strong channel noise.

Figure 6 presents the data for the Front Left and Front Right of the chosen channel, illustrating the wheel center's movement in the Z direction. It is evident that the Front Left exhibits considerably more noise compared to the Front Right. Theoretically, this implies that the amplitudes on the left side should be higher than those on the right side in the frequency ranges where the noise occurs.

Conducting a Fourier analysis on the aforementioned channel verifies the hypothesis that amplitude variations exist across different frequencies. There is a noticeable increase in amplitude for frequencies up to 10 hertz. The initial peak is insignificant, as it represents the very slow fundamental oscillation of the signal. Consequently, only frequencies above roughly 1 Hz are pertinent to these considerations.

By utilizing these insights, one can determine the average value from the dataset generated by diff() and subsequently compare the values for both sides. Additionally, the percentage difference between the two channels can be calculated, and an alert can be issued if the discrepancy is excessively large.

NaN in MATLAB stands for "Not a Number" - it is a special floating-point value that represents undefined or unrepresentable numerical results. Common Causes of NaN:

NaN values often indicate:

- Sensor malfunction or disconnection
- Data transmission errors
- Out-of-range measurements
- Calibration failures
- Signal processing errors

The measurement data, now devoid of NaN values, is assigned to a new variable. An array of the same length as the measurement data is generated, containing only zeros and ones. A one indicates where interpolation has occurred. The count of interpolated values is then determined and recorded in a table for reference. In this scenario, the missing measurement data is interpolated using a linear method.

This section brings up another crucial issue: how should one handle measurement data with excessive missing values? To address this, a query was integrated into the main script. It utilizes the calculated number of NaN values from the completeness check function to terminate the program once the percentage hits 17%. Beyond this percentage, linear interpolation issues may arise if the missing values are located at specific points, such as the peaks and troughs of the measurement data. The situation worsens if they are concentrated in a single area.

The subsequent step involves executing the Fourier transform using the fft() function. The algorithm's calculations and the individual steps for executing them were sourced from the Matlab help (MathWorks, 2022) and tailored to meet the requirements.

A Fourier transform is conducted for both channels at the same time, as they need to be compared. Additionally, the amplitude is normalized, which does not affect the results since it is applied to both sides. Moreover, the spectrum must be adjusted, and the frequency array calculated. This is performed following the example on the Matlab help page (MathWorks, 2022).

Following this, a condition is applied to identify the position of the 1 Hz frequency. This value is used to eliminate all amplitudes before the frequency and to ascertain the difference between the remaining values, providing their amplitudes. The mean of the absolute values is then computed to determine their dimensions.

The process involves first identifying the larger mean value and then dividing it by the smaller mean value, utilizing an if condition to achieve this. The resulting value is subsequently recorded in the results table and displayed as output.

## V. Outline of the Results

In the following, the results are outlined, the advantages and disadvantages of the proposed solution are discussed and some of the areas in which it is applicable are given.

The objective of this scientific study, which was to develop a functional algorithm for identifying a range of errors on the Suspension Motion Simulator, has been accomplished. Additionally, a concept has been devised to enable future expansion of the program to identify more errors. The algorithm created here allows for an initial diagnosis of the data in real-time or during measurement and can be repeated if an error occurs. The algorithm is adaptable to the tests conducted through extensive parameterization, which, among other things, facilitates highly accurate jump detection.

An important benefit of the developed algorithm is its versatility across various data sets, along with the ability to manage dynamic measurements, as long as they fulfill the required criteria. Additionally, the inclusion of multiple editable lists facilitates the enhancement of the algorithm's capabilities. Should future modifications to the different channels be needed, they can be easily incorporated by updating these lists. This establishes a robust basis for creating a database with accurate measurement data or for later eliminating flawed data sets. Consequently, we can continue to pursue the objective of integrating machine learning into test bench evaluation. Moreover, the evaluation process now requires less time, allowing us to use this time to, for instance, redo incorrect measurements. This also helps achieve the aim of cutting costs and easing the workload of the test bench team and clients.

To summarize, the paper's primary contributions include the creation of effective algorithms for edge computing platforms that assess sensor data quality during production processes. This is achieved through a structured methodology, exemplified by the Suspension Motion Simulator case study, which validates methods for enhancing sensor quality using quantifiable performance metrics. The research posits that unified quality assessment strategies can adeptly manage various sensor technologies from different manufacturers, each with distinct protocols and data formats, and that sensor errors exhibit identifiable patterns detectable through mathematical techniques such as Fourier analysis and statistical thresholds. However, the approach has some limitations; the validation is mainly centered on errors in the Aramis SRX optical measurement system, which may not fully represent the range of sensor failures in diverse CPPS environments. Despite the automation objectives, the system still necessitates human oversight for decisions regarding measurement repetition. Additionally, the paper does not thoroughly explore the challenges of integrating with existing industrial monitoring systems beyond basic compatibility.

## VI. Conclusion and Future Work

This study has effectively created and confirmed detailed methods to enhance the quality of sensor data in CPPS, including error detection by utilizing digitalization technologies. The structured framework offered tackles essential issues in contemporary manufacturing settings by merging cutting-edge digital technologies with practical implementation factors. The newly developed methodology showcases notable advancements in sensor reliability by employing real-time quality assessment algorithms, multi-modal error detection capabilities, and smooth integration with current production infrastructures. The Suspension Motion Simulator case study confirms the practical effectiveness of these methods, demonstrating significant improvements in the accuracy of sensor fault detection and a decrease in false alarm rates. The framework's modular design allows for scalable deployment across various manufacturing settings while maintaining computational efficiency suitable for edge computing platforms.

There are numerous promising avenues that warrant further investigation. To begin with, the fusion of artificial intelligence and large language models offers transformative possibilities for managing sensor data quality. Foundation models, pre-trained on a variety of sensor datasets, could deliver universal anomaly detection capabilities across diverse sensor networks, while transformer-based architectures might capture intricate temporal dependencies in sensor time-series data that traditional methods overlook. Large language models could automate the creation of sensor maintenance documentation, translate complex sensor anomalies into human-readable diagnostic reports, and offer conversational interfaces for interactive sensor troubleshooting. The foundation established by this research provides a robust platform for continued advancement in sensor data quality management, positioning manufacturers to leverage digitalization technologies for enhanced production reliability and competitiveness in Industry 4.0 environments.

## Acknowledgement

This research was partially funded by the German Federal Ministry for Economic Affairs and Climate Protection (BMWK) in the funding guideline "Digitization of the vehicle manufacturers and supplier industry" in the funding framework "Future investments in vehicle manufacturers and the supplier industry", financed by the European Union, and supervised by the project sponsor VDI Technologiezentrum GmbH within the joint research project "Werk 4.0" (grant number 13IK022K). Furthermore, it was partially funded by the German Federal Ministry of Economics and Technology through the AiF as part of the program "Central Innovation Program for SMEs" based on a resolution of the German Bundestag within the project "PreMaMisch-Predictive-Maintenance-Systems for Mixing Plants" (grant number KK5023201LT0), by the German Federal Ministry of Education and Research (BMBF) within the project "PAL-PerspektiveArbeitLausitz" (grant number 02L19C301) and by the BMBF in the funding program "Zukunft der Wertschöpfung - Forschung zu Produktion Dienstleistung und Arbeit" within the project "ProKI" (grant number 02P22A050).

## REFERENCES


[1] L. Monostori, "Cyber-physical production systems: Roots, expectations and r&d challenges," *Procedia cirp*, vol. 17, pp. 9–13, 2014, retrieved: September 2025. [Online]. Available: https://www.sciencedirect.com/science/article/pii/S2212827114003497

[2] Cyber-Physical Production Systems. Copyright ©Connected Everything II. Retrieved: September 2025. [Online]. Available: https://connectedeverything.ac.uk/cyber-physical-production-systems-2/

[3] S. Marathe, A. Nambi, M. Swaminathan, and R. Sutaria, "Currentsense: A novel approach for fault and drift detection in environmental iot sensors," in *Proceedings of the international conference on internet-of-things design and implementation*, 2021, pp. 93–105, retrieved: September 2025. [Online]. Available: https://www.microsoft.com/en-us/research/wp-content/uploads/2021/05/CurrentSense-Akshay-iotdi2021.pdf

[4] K. Ramesh *et al.*, "Comparison and assessment of machine learning approaches in manufacturing applications," *Industrial Artificial Intelligence*, vol. 3, no. 1, p. 2, 2025, retrieved: September 2025. [Online]. Available: https://link.springer.com/article/10.1007/s44244-025-00023-3

[5] A. Saeed, M. A. Khan, U. Akram, W. J. Obidallah, S. Jawed, and A. Ahmad, "Deep learning based approaches for intelligent industrial machinery health management and fault diagnosis in resource-constrained environments," *Scientific Reports*, vol. 15, no. 1, p. 1114, 2025, retrieved: September 2025. [Online]. Available: https://www.nature.com/articles/s41598-024-79151-2

[6] H. E. Ahmed and M. Al Mubarak, *Roles of Big Data and AI in Manufacturing*. Cham: Springer Nature Switzerland, 2024, pp. 3–25, retrieved: September 2025. [Online]. Available: https://doi.org/10.1007/978-3-031-71649-2_1

[7] Industrial Edge Computing Megatrends: Special Report Technology July 23, 2024. Copyright ©Connected Everything II. Retrieved: September 2025. [Online]. Available: https://iebmedia.com/technology/edge-cloud/industrial-edge-computing-megatrends-special-report/

[8] H. Wiemer, A. Dementyev, and S. Ihlenfeldt, "A holistic quality assurance approach for machine learning applications in cyber-physical production systems," *Applied Sciences*, vol. 11, no. 20, 2021. [Online]. Available: https://www.mdpi.com/2076-3417/11/20/9590

[9] L. B. Magalas and A. Piłat, "Zero-point drift in low-frequency mechanical spectroscopy," *Solid State Phenomena*, vol. 115, pp. 285–292, 2006, retrieved: September 2025. [Online]. Available: https://www.researchgate.net/publication/243761190_Zero-Point_Drift_in_Low-Frequency_Mechanical_Spectroscopy

[10] G. Müller and G. Sberveglieri, "Origin of baseline drift in metal oxide gas sensors: Effects of bulk equilibration," *Chemosensors*, vol. 10, no. 5, p. 171, 2022, retrieved: September 2025. [Online]. Available: https://www.mdpi.com/2227-9040/10/5/171

[11] APERIO, "Identifying and managing risks of sensor drift," March 2025, Copyright ©2025 APERIO | Site by Halibut Blue. Retrieved: September 2025. [Online]. Available: https://aperio.ai/sensor-drift/

[12] G. Tancev, "Relevance of drift components and unit-to-unit variability in the predictive maintenance of low-cost electrochemical sensor systems," *Sensors*, vol. 21, no. 9, p. 3298, 2021, retrieved: September 2025. [Online]. Available: https://pmc.ncbi.nlm.nih.gov/articles/PMC8126229/

[13] Zero Point Error of Pressure Sensor. Copyright ©2023 Eastsensor Technology. Retrieved: September 2025. [Online]. Available: https://www.eastsensor.com/blog/zero-point-error-of-pressure-sensor/

[14] R. Laref, D. Ahmadou, E. Losson, and M. Siadat, "Orthogonal Signal Correction to Improve Stability Regression Model in Gas Sensor Systems," *Journal of Sensors*, vol. 2017, no. 1, p. 9851406, 2017, retrieved: September 2025. [Online]. Available: https://www.hindawi.com/journals/js/2017/9851406/

[15] ZERO INSTRUMENT, "Sensor drift: Causes, mechanisms, and effective compensation methods," April 2025, Copyright ©2025 Just Measure it. Retrieved: September 2025. [Online]. Available: https://zeroinstrument.com/sensor-drift-causes-mechanisms-and-effective-compensation-methods/

[16] A. Rudnitskaya, "Calibration Update and Drift Correction for Electronic Noses and Tongues," *Frontiers in chemistry*, vol. 6, p. 433, 2018, retrieved: September 2025. [Online]. Available: https://pmc.ncbi.nlm.nih.gov/articles/PMC6167416/

[17] Sensitivity Drift. Copyright ©2025 or its licensors and contributors. Retrieved: September 2025. [Online]. Available: https://www.sciencedirect.com/topics/engineering/sensitivity-drift

[18] S. B. Noor, "Heterogeneous Sensor Networks: Challenges and Future Research Directions," *EDUZONE International Peer Reviewed Journal*, vol. 9, no. 2, 2020, retrieved: September 2025. [Online]. Available: https://www.researchgate.net/publication/372188516_Heterogeneous_Sensor_Networks_Challenges_and_Future_Research_Directions

[19] S. Munirathinam, "Drift detection analytics for iot sensors," *Procedia Computer Science*, vol. 180, pp. 903–912, 2021, retrieved: September 2025. [Online]. Available: https://www.sciencedirect.com/science/article/pii/S1877050921003951

[20] C. C. Aggarwal, "An introduction to outlier analysis," in *Outlier analysis*. Springer, 2016, pp. 1–34, retrieved: September 2025. [Online]. Available: https://link.springer.com/book/10.1007/978-3-319-47578-3

[21] M. Olteanu, F. Rossi, and F. Yger, "Meta-survey on outlier and anomaly detection," *Neurocomputing*, vol. 555, p. 126634, 2023, retrieved: September 2025. [Online]. Available: https://www.sciencedirect.com/science/article/pii/S0925231223007579

[22] Sensor Calibration Drift. Copyright ©2024 Sustainability Directory. Retrieved: September 2025. [Online]. Available: https://pollution.sustainability-directory.com/term/sensor-calibration-drift/

[23] B. D. Hansen, T. B. Hansen, T. B. Moeslund, and D. G. Jensen, "Data-driven drift detection in real process tanks: Bridging the gap between academia and practice," *Water*, vol. 14, no. 6, p. 926, 2022, retrieved: September 2025. [Online]. Available: https://www.mdpi.com/2073-4441/14/6/926

[24] What Causes Zero and Span Offset in Pressure Transducers? Copyright ©2025 Ashcroft, Inc. All Rights Reserved. Retrieved: September 2025. [Online]. Available: https://blog.ashcroft.com/what-causes-zero-and-span-offset-in-pressure-transducers

[25] What is Total Error Band & How do You Calculate It? Copyright ©2025 Setra Systems. All Rights Reserved. Retrieved: September 2025. [Online]. Available: https://www.setra.com/blog/what-is-total-error-band-and-how-do-you-calculate-it

[26] Y. Pei, Z. Qian, B. Jing, D. Kang, and L. Zhang, "Data-driven method for wind turbine yaw angle sensor zero-point shifting fault detection," *Energies*, vol. 11, no. 3, p. 553, 2018, retrieved: September 2025. [Online]. Available: https://www.mdpi.com/1996-1073/11/3/553

[27] UNDERSTANDING AND MINIMISING ADC CONVERSION ERRORS. Copyright ©2003 STMicroelectronics - All Rights Reserved. Retrieved: September 2025. [Online]. Available: https://www.st.com/resource/en/application_note/an1636-understanding-and-minimising-adc-conversion-errors-stmicroelectronics.pdf

[28] E. Dwobeng, "Measuring bit errors in the output word of an a/d converter," *Application Note of Texas Instruments, SLAA582*, pp. 1–10, 2013, retrieved: September 2025. [Online]. Available: https://e2echina.ti.com/cfs-file/__key/telligent-evolution-components-attachments/13-109-00-00-00-00-94-70/Measuring-Bit-Errors-in-the-Output-Word-of-an-Analog_2D00_to_2D00_Digital-Converter.pdf

[29] A. O'Grady. Transducer/Sensor Excitation and Measurement Techniques. Copyright ©2025 Analog Devices, Inc. All Rights Reserved. Retrieved: September 2025. [Online]. Available: https://www.analog.com/en/resources/analog-dialogue/articles/transducer-sensor-excitation-and-measurement-techniques.html

[30] M. Pota, G. De Pietro, and M. Esposito, "Real-time anomaly detection on time series of industrial furnaces: A comparison of autoencoder architectures," *Engineering Applications of Artificial Intelligence*, vol. 124, p. 106597, 2023, retrieved: September 2025. [Online]. Available: https://www.sciencedirect.com/science/article/pii/S0952197623007819

[31] H. Zumbahlen. Staying Well Grounded. Copyright ©2025 Analog Devices, Inc. All Rights Reserved. Retrieved: September 2025. [Online]. Available: https://www.analog.com/en/resources/analog-dialogue/articles/staying-well-grounded.html

[32] Measurement Fundamentals. Copyright ©2025 NATIONAL INSTRUMENTS CORP. ALL RIGHTS RESERVED. Retrieved: September 2025. [Online]. Available: https://www.ni.com/en/shop/data-acquisition/measurement-fundamentals.html

[33] Z. Liu, Z. Sun, G. Shi, J. Wu, and X. Xie, "A novel algorithm for online spike detection," in *MATEC Web of Conferences*, vol. 173. EDP Sciences, 2018, p. 02017, retrieved: September 2025. [Online]. Available: https://www.matec-conferences.org/articles/matecconf/pdf/2018/32/matecconf_smima2018_02017.pdf

[34] Y. Zhang and K. Rasmussen, "Detection of electromagnetic interference attacks on sensor systems," in *2020 IEEE Symposium on Security and Privacy (SP)*. IEEE, 2020, pp. 203–216, retrieved: September 2025. [Online]. Available: https://ieeexplore.ieee.org/iel7/9144328/9152199/09152793.pdf

[35] W. Zhang, L. Qin, R. Chen, J. Wang, W. Zheng, and W. Zhou, "The influence mechanism and improvement strategy of multiplexer on measurement error of the 2-d resistive sensor array data acquisition circuit," *IEEE Sensors Journal*, vol. 23, no. 17, pp. 20 086–20 096, 2023, retrieved: September 2025. [Online]. Available: https://ieeexplore.ieee.org/iel7/7361/4427201/10198481.pdf

[36] M. Zinner *et al.*, "Contributions to an FMEA/FMSA Based Methodology to Improve Data Quality of Cyber Physical Production Systems Through Digitalisation: a Use Case Approach," *INTELLI 2025*, pp. 59–69, 2025, retrieved: September 2025. [Online]. Available: https://www.thinkmind.org/articles/intelli_2025_2_60_60028.pdf

[37] J. A. Carter, A. I. Barros, J. A. Nóbrega, and G. L. Donati, "Traditional Calibration Methods in Atomic Spectrometry and New Calibration Strategies for Inductively Coupled Plasma Mass Spectrometry," *Frontiers in Chemistry*, vol. 6, p. 504, 2018, retrieved: September 2025. [Online]. Available: https://doi.org/10.3389/fchem.2018.00504

[38] Y. Zhang, L. O. H. Wijeratne, S. Talebi, and D. J. Lary, "Machine learning for light sensor calibration," *Sensors*, vol. 21, no. 18, p. 6259, 2021, retrieved: September 2025. [Online]. Available: https://doi.org/10.3390/s21186259

[39] S. Y. Hayoun *et al.*, "Physics and semantic informed multi-sensor calibration via optimization theory and self-supervised learning," *Scientific Reports*, vol. 14, p. 2541, 2024, retrieved: September 2025. [Online]. Available: https://doi.org/10.1038/s41598-024-53009-z

[40] Y.-K. Li *et al.*, "Outlier detection for multivariate calibration in near infrared spectroscopic analysis by model diagnostics," *Chinese Journal of Analytical Chemistry*, vol. 44, no. 2, pp. 184–189, 2016, retrieved: September 2025. [Online]. Available: https://www.sciencedirect.com/science/article/abs/pii/S1872204016609076

[41] Y. Zhao *et al.*, "PyOD 2: A Python Library for Outlier Detection with LLM-powered Model Selection," 2024, retrieved: September 2025. [Online]. Available: https://arxiv.org/abs/2412.12154

[42] Y. Zhao, Z. Nasrullah, and Z. Li, "Pyod: A python toolbox for scalable outlier detection," *Journal of Machine Learning Research*, vol. 20, pp. 1–7, 2019, retrieved: September 2025. [Online]. Available: https://www.jmlr.org/papers/volume20/19-011/19-011.pdf

[43] P. Meschke, "Konzeptentwicklung zur automatisierten Messdatenanalyse hinsichtlich Fehlererkennung und -kategorisierung am Suspension Motion Simulator; English: Concept development for automated measurement data analysis with regard to fault detection and categorisation on the suspension motion simulator," 2022, internal unplished study; TU-Dresden.